Jim Vopat

Writing Circles

Kids Revolutionize Workshop

HEINEMANN
Portsmouth, NH

Heinemann
361 Hanover Street
Portsmouth, NH 03801–3912
www.heinemann.com

Offices and agents throughout the world

© 2009 by Jim Vopat

Library of Congress Cataloging-in-Publication Data
Vopat, James.
  Writing circles : kids revolutionize workshop / Jim Vopat.
     p. cm.
  Includes bibliographical references and index.
  ISBN-13: 978-0-325-01746-4
  ISBN-10: 0-325-01746-8
  1. English language—Composition and exercises—Study and teaching. 2. Writers' workshops. 3. Student-centered learning. I. Title.
  LB1576.V67 2009
  808'.042071—dc21   2009020453

Editor: Harvey Daniels
Production editor: Patricia Adams
Typesetter: Pear Graphic Design
Cover design: Lisa Fowler
Interior design: Joyce Weston
Manufacturing: Steve Bernier

Printed in the United States of America on acid-free paper
13 12 11 10 09 VP 1 2 3 4 5

Contents

Foreword

Recently, I've had a chance to watch Jim Vopat introduce writing circles to groups of teachers. It always unfolds the same way. As Jim outlines the structure and then engages teachers in trying it for themselves, people start to smile. The conversational volume in the room gradually rises, as people share their writing, laugh, and say things like: "Whoa, this is really cool." "I never thought of this." "This is really different." And "My kids would totally love this activity."

Writing Circles is that elusive something new under the sun, a genuine departure and an exciting step ahead. It's what's next. And it is also something big.

On the surface, what Jim has done is take the successful model of literature circles— which might be concisely defined as small, peer-led reading discussion groups—and created a parallel structure for composition. Instead of kids picking a common book to read and discuss in groups, they choose a common *topic* to write about, and each person creates original text in whatever genre and style they prefer. Then, groups meet to share, celebrate, and give each other helpful, constructive responses. Periodically, students choose one draft to develop further, and the group morphs into an author's support team, serving as agents, editors, and publishers.

If you are already using literature circles or book clubs in your classroom, you will immediately see this as a fresh and engaging adaptation. But, as Chicago teacher Nancy Steineke says in the book, there's much more here than novelty and enjoyment:

> A writing circle is much more than a fun variation. This is a whole new kind of writing workshop. The kids get more useful feedback in their writing circles than they do from individual conferences with me. I kind of hate to say that—I grew up with the original workshop model, where the key structure is one-to-one conferences with the teacher. But with writing circles, I see the kids' writing progressing faster than it does when I am the main source of feedback. The power comes from the audience, I think. Having three or

four other kids as an immediate audience, peers who care about you and attend to your every word and will give you honest feedback—that's the driving motivation, instead of teacher approval or grades.

What? Those short one-to-one, teacher-kid conferences that we struggle so hard to cram into our busy writing classes might not matter as much as we thought? Could it be that young writers can grow even more effectively in well-structured, kid-led teams?

But wait. Our student writing groups haven't always worked so well, have they? For many years, we teachers have struggled to perfect what we used to call "peer editing groups." Now, with *Writing Circles*, we have a fully elaborated structure for the whole process; that helps kids support each other at all stages, from topic selection and drafting, through thoughtful revision, and onward to sharing and publication. Jim's subtitle is no overstatement: this is how *Kids Revolutionize Workshop*.

This book is just the latest in a string of Jim's special contributions to our field.

- In an era when teacher minilessons too often morph into endless, lumbering maxi-lessons (read: the return of lecturing), Jim gave us a practical corrective in his 2007 book: *Microlessons in Writing*, a set of 75 one-page structures that brings out the best in student writers K–12.
- Jim has created a whole body of work—books, videos, and workshops — about parent involvement in schools, especially in neighborhoods with poor, minority families who are reticent to get involved. The key to Jim's amazing Parent Project program: invite adults into workshop style learning, just like their kids enjoy in the classroom.
- Jim has been a Fulbright scholar, studying and helping to improve educational systems in India and Sri Lanka.
- Jim has curated spectacular exhibits of children's art in a large Milwaukee gallery. These well-attended shows taught adults who work outside schools what priceless and original art gets made every day in American classrooms.

Allow me to introduce you to a very special voice in our field, Jim Vopat, a true renaissance educator. And welcome to something really new, energizing, and transformative. Welcome to *Writing Circles*.

Harvey "Smokey" Daniels
Santa Fe, NM

Contributing Teachers

Primary K–2

Jennifer McDonell
Randall Elementary,
Waukesha, WI

Intermediate

Tom Brown, Literacy Coach
Morgandale School,
Milwaukee, WI

Deborah Zaffiro, Literacy Coach
Tippecanoe School for the Arts
and Humanities, Milwaukee, WI

Jane Borden, Gr. 5–6
Tippecanoe School for the Arts
and Humanities, Milwaukee, WI

Matthew Stark, Gr. 4
Tippecanoe School for the Arts
and Humanities, Milwaukee, WI

Andrea Payan, Gr. 4–5
Morgandale School,
Milwaukee, WI

Abigail Plummer, Gr. 4
Tippecanoe School for the Arts
and Humanities, Milwaukee, WI

Middle School

Joan LoPresti, Writing Specialist,
Gr. 6–8
Henry W. Longfellow School,
Milwaukee, WI

Melissa Schmidt, Gr. 7
Kennedy Middle School,
Germantown, WI

Nona Schrader, Gr. 8
Jefferson Middle School,
Jefferson, WI

Jody Henderson-Sykes, Gr. 7–8
Fernwood Montessori,
Milwaukee, WI

High School

Nancy Steineke, Gr. 9–10
Victor J. Andrew High School,
Tinley Park, IL

University

Elise Riepenhoff, Milwaukee
Writing Project, Carroll University,
Waukesha, WI

The Tao of Writing Circles

Writing Circles?

Groups of four to six kids—some gathered around tables, some sitting on pillows on the floor, two groups out in the hall. The Mall Monkeys are furthest down the hall; the Penguins—some sitting, some standing—settle in just outside the classroom door. Los Viejitos, Smooth Operators, and Purple People Eaters sit around tables in classroom corners, listening to one of the other members of their group read their work. Silver Snakes are on pillows near the windows meeting with their teacher, excited to hear he's written about unknowingly making camp on a huge anthill. The Femme Lattes have pushed desks together at the front of the classroom and are one-upping each other on the topic "why we should be able to have cell phones in school." Los Viejitos' topic is "favorite animal"; "friends" for the Smooth Operators; "when I grow up" for Purple People Eaters; "music" for the Mall Monkeys; "bugs" for the Silver Snakes; and "shipwrecked on an island with your worst enemy" for the Penguins. Each Penguin has approached the topic in a unique way: a struggle for survival, provisional reconciliation, epitaph, some gore, an unexpected letter to a friend who moved away, rescue by cruise boat. After listening to each draft, the Penguins practice the day's response strategy called *point out*: "Tell the writer one thing you liked. *Point out* something interesting."

What are all these students in the middle of? Writing circles. Small groups of students meeting regularly to share drafts, choose common writing topics, practice positive response, and, in general, help each other become better writers. The writing circle dynamic includes the following steps:

- Groups of kids name their writing circle and choose their group's writing topic.
- Kids write on this topic, using any format or genre.
- Writing circle minilessons focus on circle management and writing craft.

- Writing circles meet.
- Kids share their writing.
- Kids respond to one another's writing.
- Each circle chooses their next writing topic.
- New topics and some writing from each circle are shared with the whole class.
- Kids think about the writing circle sessions they've just completed and jot down their reflections and notes in their writing circle notebook.
- Periodically, kids review their rough pieces and select the most promising one to revise.
- Writers participate in a circle devoted to collaborative revision, editing, and publication.
- Classmates serve as one another's agents, illustrators, reviewers, and editors.
- Finished works are shared and celebrated in some public form.

Writing circles are a fun, low risk opportunity to "just write." Kids freely and spontaneously explore questions or subjects that fascinate them—any topic or issue within a particular subject. While the small groups do choose common topics, individual kids in the group decide which genre (poem, story, letter, blog) and approach, stance, and specific subject matter suit them best. Then, after getting plenty of guidance on how to give friendly feedback, they share their drafts in a positive, supportive context. Participating in this process helps students shed their fear of the blank page, build fluency, develop confidence, learn content, and explore the various text structures they can draw on as writers.

If you're familiar with literature circles, writing circles need less introduction. Literature circles have revitalized many classrooms by giving kids choice in what they read and authentic structures for meaningful and engaged peer-led discussion. As Harvey Daniels defines the strategy in the second edition of *Literature Circles,*

> Literature Circles are small, peer-led discussion groups whose members have chosen to read the same story, poem, article, or book. While reading each group-assigned portion of the text (either in or outside of class), members make notes to help them contribute to the upcoming discussion, and everyone comes to the group with ideas to share. Each group

follows a reading and meeting schedule, holding periodic discussions on the way through the book. When they finish a book, the circle members may share highlights of their reading with the wider community. (2002, 2)

The structure of writing circles mirrors that of literature circles, with kids' writing serving as the text. In writing circles, small groups of kids write on an agreed topic, share and discuss their drafts, receive positive response, choose a new writing idea, and end with a brief reflection. When compared to the eleven "key ingredients" of literature circles that Daniels lists (2002, 18), the parallels one can see between literature circles and writing circles emphasize how important student choice and small-group collaboration are to learning.

Even if you're unfamiliar with literature circles, much of the writing circle dynamic is similar to writing workshop, your own participation in a writer's group, or what you've heard from someone you know who belongs to a writer's group. Adult writers groups are as abundant and pervasive as adult reading groups (although perhaps not as visible, since Oprah hasn't featured any on her show). Don't you know someone in a writing group (or someone who knows someone)?

Writers sharing and talking about what they have written with other writers has likely been happening for as long as people have been writing. As Anne Ruggles Gere puts it in *Writing Groups: History, Theory, and Implications*, "Writers have always asked friends and colleagues for feedback" (1987, 22). For famous authors as well as kids reading stories they've written to each other, there is something immensely satisfying in sharing writing and getting a response.

From Virginia Woolf's famous Bloomsbury group to the third-grade Peanut Butter Jellies sharing their stories in their circle of desks by the windows, writing groups are an historic and enduring component of writing. Just Google "writing groups" and view their long history and abundance: the Diversity Writer's Group for Men, River Voices, Turning Point, League of Extra Ordinary Revisionists, Dreaming in Ink, the Word Painters, and the Yet Unnamed. Small town, big town, rural, suburban, urban, every state, every country, worldwide.

Writers groups come in many forms—in and out of school. Literary salons, peer revision groups, helping circles, author collectives, therapy sessions, writing workshop share sessions, peer review and peer editing groups, writers linked by geography or theme or genre, in person or on line,

Literature Circles	Writing Circles
Kids choose their own reading materials.	Through consensus, each group chooses a writing topic. Each student decides how he or she will write about the topic.
Small temporary groups form based on book choice.	Small temporary groups reach consensus on a common writing topic.
Different groups read different books.	Different groups write on different topics.
Groups meet on a regular, predictable schedule to discuss their reading.	Groups meet on a regular, predictable schedule to share and discuss their writing.
Kids use written or drawn notes to guide both their reading and discussion.	Kids use structured ways to share, respond, and discuss their writing.
Discussion topics come from the students.	The type of response that guides discussion comes from the kids and is usually initiated by the writer.
Group meetings aim to be open, natural conversations about books, so personal connections, digressions, and open-ended questions are welcome.	In group meetings, kids have relaxed, supportive conversations about their writing. There's a spirit of community and collaboration.
The teacher serves as a facilitator, not a group member or instructor.	The teacher serves primarily as a facilitator, and when possible participates in a group.
Evaluation is by teacher observation and student self-evaluation.	Evaluation is through teacher observation, kids' "think–back" reflections, and documentation of "good faith effort."
A spirit of playfulness and fun pervades the room.	Kids are interested in how other kids write about the agreed-on topic— they laugh, clap, or listen in silent suspense. They are engaged in the joy of sharing and responding to writing.
When books are finished, readers share with their classmates and then new groups form around new reading choices.	After writing a good number of drafts, kids choose all or part of one to develop, revise, edit, and publish. Each writing circle becomes a publishing circle.

voluntarily and involuntarily. What connects them all is the sharing/ response dynamic, the positive paradox of the solitary writer as collaborative participant.

The nature of writing groups is connected to the purpose of the writing group—the reason that has brought the writers together. Is the purpose to help improve participant writing, provide an audience, learn how to adhere to genre conventions, focus on details of language and structure, provide emotional support, or network with publishing professionals?

According to Gere (1987, 3), writing groups have three defining features: (1) *immediate response* (instead of waiting for the teacher's written comments), (2) from an *audience*, (3) affirming the *social aspect of writing* ("tangible evidence that writing involves human interaction as well as solitary inscription").

For many teachers, writing groups are associated with the work of Peter Elbow, Ken Macrorie, Donald Graves, Lucy Calkins, and Nancie Atwell, although the term takes on somewhat different meanings for each of them. In writing workshop classrooms, writing groups are an integral part of the recurrent structure—from "receiving" drafts to final peer editing and publishing. They often become carefully structured peer conferencing and response groups. In the most recent edition of *The Art of Teaching Writing* (1994), for example, Lucy Calkins lists "peer conferring and/or response groups" as one of the five essential components of writing workshop (the others being mini-lessons, work time, whole-class share sessions, and publication celebrations) (188–91). As described by Calkins, response groups meet "almost daily for at least twenty minutes" with the group serving "mostly as a sounding board" for the writer. "Response groups are usually formed by students at the teacher's suggestion, and there are usually four or five members in a response group."

As kids move up through the grades, writing groups have tended to take on a more critical dimension, to the point that, in graduate school, writing groups often feature negative "critiques" from which some members never fully recover. For many older student writers, the invitation to "get into a group and critique one another's writing" sends a chill down the spine. Most kids aren't looking forward to their writing being "critiqued"—especially when it is a draft.

As valuable as they *can* be, writing response groups are largely underutilized in classrooms. When push comes to shove in our time-and-test-driven contemporary classrooms, "group response" is often the first component of writing workshop to be shortened or abandoned.

Writing circles restore group response to its essential place in the writing process. In contrast to "critiques," writing circles are all about confidence, fluency, joy, and delight. In writing circles, kids expect to be listened to and enjoy being listened to. Because students often write about new topics in new ways, writing circles continue to challenge students to take their writing to the next level while remaining low risk, friendly, and supportive. When kids form writing circles they become part of a history and movement for writers, by writers.

Why Writing Circles?

Writing circles help kids become better writers through a recurrent workshop structure that defines an ongoing supportive audience, honors and develops writing "voice," encourages experimentation and collaboration, and rehabilitates the writing wounded through low-risk writing experiences. Go Penguins! Go Silver Snakes! Go Smooth Operators!

The Missing Link

Writing circles don't just happen but exist within the framework of a balanced writing program. What exactly constitutes a "balanced" writing program depends on how the word *balanced* is defined. In *Invitations* (1991), Regie Routman defines a balanced writing program as an interplay of four "approaches": writing aloud (teacher models as she thinks aloud), shared writing (teacher and students write together), guided writing (writing workshop, small-group instruction), and independent writing (writing "without teacher intervention or evaluation"—including writing to learn and freewriting). In their comprehensive language and literacy framework, Irene Fountas and Gay Sue Pinnell (2000) exclude writing to learn but add investigations ("students pose original questions that form the basis of research)." The "6 + 1 Traits" writing framework uses a common language to create a "common vision" of good writing (ideas, organization, voice, word choice, sentence fluency, conventions, and presentation). Through the 6 + 1 model, teachers and students "pinpoint areas of strength and weakness as they continue to focus on improved writing."

In addition, it makes sense to consider other aspects of balance: balance between teacher-guided and student-directed approaches, between informal drafts and polished pieces, and in the kind of social interaction kids experience with their writing. "Balance" can then be visualized as "parallel continuums," to use Daniels's phrase (2002, 28):

Student directed		teacher directed
Individual	small group	whole group
Informal drafts pieces		crafted and assessed

How writing activities play out varies from classroom to classroom, teacher to teacher. That said, given their basic characteristics, here's a sense of how major writing approaches/activities—including writing circles—sort out on the continuums:

Student directed		teacher directed
Independent writing, writing to learn, investigations, writing circles, writing workshop		writing aloud, 6 + 1 Traits, shared writing, whole-class writing

Individual	small group	whole group
Independent writing, writing to learn, writing workshop investigations	writing circles	writing aloud, whole-class writing, 6 + 1 Traits, shared writing

Informal drafts		crafted and assessed pieces
Independent writing, writing to learn, writing workshop	writing circles	investigations, whole-class writing, 6 + 1 Traits

Writing circles are the missing link: "missing" because what's largely missing from the current balanced writing program is an ongoing collaborative writing structure, "link" because writing circles combine collaborative small-group work with self-sponsored writing in a workshop format.

Just as literature circles provide a structure for independent reading in small groups, writing circles provide small-group independent writing. *The bottom line is there are only two delivery systems for independent writing— writing independently in the classic workshop format and writing circles.* Writing circles provide a structure for a neglected part of what kids need to become better writers: independent small-group collaboration to motivate and support self-sponsored student-directed writing.

At what grade levels do writing circles "work"? The examples in this book range from second grade to graduate school. If writing workshop or literature circles "work" with your kids, so will writing circles. As teachers, we make the necessary developmental adjustments—smaller circles and shorter time periods in the early elementary grades, for example. In a way it's more a question of kids being comfortable with group work and sharing drafts than grade level (see Chapters 4 and 5).

Writing Circles and Writing Workshop

Writing circles revolutionize writing workshop by harnessing the power of kids to help each other become better writers. Kids working together animates the basic writing circle rhythm of topic selection, drafting, sharing drafts, and constructive response. In writing circles kids not only write a lot; they also talk a lot to each other about writing, about topics, about different ways to develop an idea. Ever exhaust yourself trying to conference one-on-one with every kid's writing? It's impossible if they are writing every day. And yet kids need to write everyday and get specific supportive response. In writing circles, this happens through kids conferencing with kids. This frees the teacher to participate in writing circles as well and to conference one-on-one when they can.

There's certainly much writing workshop here. Writing circles would not exist without writing workshop. There's a shared belief in kid-selected independent writing, conferencing, minilessons, and the inherent worth of moving from draft through revision and editing to finished work. What's revolutionary about writing circles is that small groups of kids work *in an ongoing collaboration* to make writing workshop happen. The circle drafts kids write are individual and independent, and each kid responds to the chosen topic in their own way—whatever genre, style, or point of view. And yet the writing clearly exists within the community of the other kids in the writing circle. Kids move quickly from draft to draft but each draft receives a hearing (read aloud) and positive feedback. All of it by kids for kids. If we believe that all writing benefits from sharing and response, the only way we can consistently achieve this is to have kids respond and conference with each other. In writing circles kids also learn firsthand about small group dynamics: the advantages of working together to help each other write, write, write.

Let the revolution begin.

Low Risk

We are gathered here in praise of low-risk learning. As the name implies, something that's low risk has little formal consequence. For writing, low risk means kids initially write without fearing the grade or the mistake. Low risk does not mean low quality. When kids don't write for a grade, they can focus on what they think rather than spelling, wording, or punctuation. Writing can be more creative, adventurous, fun, and compelling. Peter Elbow (1997) has noted that such low risk writing "is usually livelier, clearer, and more natural—often more interesting—in spite of any carelessness and mistakes . . . I've almost never seen a piece of low-stakes writing I couldn't easily understand. But I've seen *lots* of high-stakes writing that students have worked very hard on—and found it impenetrable" (7). Writing circles are a low risk way to high-quality writing—low-risk drafts, low-risk response, and low-risk whole-class sharing—so that kids become confident and stronger writers.

Audience

Writers write for themselves but just as surely they write for readers, listeners, and an audience. In writing circles, kids often write with their audience in mind. When surveyed about their writing circle experiences, kids repeatedly mention how much they enjoy sharing their writing with a small group of other kids. The result is kids start to give extra attention in their writing to ways of engaging their potential listeners. Join a writing circle and you will hear the comic, the heartfelt, the sentimental, the rhetorical, the parable, the letter, the memoir, the inanimate point of view. Join a writing circle and because there is an audience of other kids, you will hear writing voice—distinct stylistic passages that set out to engage and entertain.

The writing circle emphasis on response from other kids provides motivation and encouragement. Other kids' drafts offer a sense of alternative writing possibilities—different points of view, genres, and stylistic flourishes. As writers, kids need to explore unfamiliar writing territories and do so in the spirit of adventure instead of in fear of error. Isn't that part of what makes a strong and resilient writer? As one student said about her writing circle experiences, "I love showing my true writing style rather than the cookie-cutter way the teachers have us write."

Collaboration

Kids do not want to write about themselves or by themselves all the time. Increasingly, we lead collaborative lives—and that includes our writing. Yet in many classrooms writing often remains solitary and competitive. Unlike the competitive classroom in which success is measured in terms of other kids' failures and writing becomes the means of sorting and grading, writing circles are collaborative and noncompetitive. In writing circles, kids work with and for one another, not against one another. Kids also come to know one another through their writing; sharing drafts becomes a bonding experience. "My circle meetings are the bomb!" says a high school sophomore. "It may seem exaggerated, but it's true. I like my group. We're all humorous people, so we work well together." Kids collaborate in selecting writing topics, responding to one another's writing, and taking on basic management responsibilities like "time keeper" and "first writer." Kids collaborate in naming their writing circle and deciding what writing to share with the entire class. In the publishing circle, kids take on framed roles to help one another improve and formalize their writing.

Many kids haven't had much experience working together—especially when it comes to writing. The keys to successful writing circle collaboration include:

- Kids feel *comfortable* writing, sharing their writing, discussing their writing, and simply working with one another.
- There are *clear guidelines* for managing the writing circle and responding to one another's writing.
- There is a *predictable structure* to the writing circle: minilesson, writing, sharing writing, new writing ideas, reflection.
- Kids *understand* what their writing circle *responsibilities* are and how to fulfill them.
- There are *mechanisms and strategies* to help kids *reach consensus* regarding topic choice and whole-class sharing of writing.

Learning by Doing

> Talking ain't knowing, right?
>> —Detective Lester Freamon on *The Wire*

> When kids do the work, they learn.
>> —Stephanie Harvey, Walloon Institute 2008 keynote
>> address

The writing circle dynamic is all about the doing—individually and as a group. In writing circles, kids decide the writing topic, they write, they share, they respond, they think of new writing ideas, they reflect on what they've learned, and they take on circle management responsibilities. After kids have written and shared numerous drafts, they choose one to revise and edit in a publishing circle. Kids keep their own records and document what they are doing and learning in their writing circle notebooks. They think back over what they've done and make meaning from it. Through all this doing, kids inevitably, playfully, define themselves as writers.

Kids as Teachers and Writers

Kids have a lot to teach one another about how to become better writers. Writing circles are a new kind of workshop that facilitates this teaching without making it seem like teaching at all. The job of a teacher of writing is to take all students to the next level: support what they are doing well and give them a way to move forward. It's a challenge for a single teacher to accomplish this one-on-one with every kid in the classroom. The teacher's very attention to their writing can feel intimidating to some kids. But when we encourage kids to teach one another, writing and writers flourish. When kids listen to one another's writing about the same topic, they all learn something about language, voice, and audience. Sometimes the learning is subtle; sometimes it's a breakthrough moment in which the writer comes to a new understanding of how language works.

Figures 1-1 through 1-5 show responses by the No Names writing circle (grades 6 to 8) to their chosen topic of "a stranger."

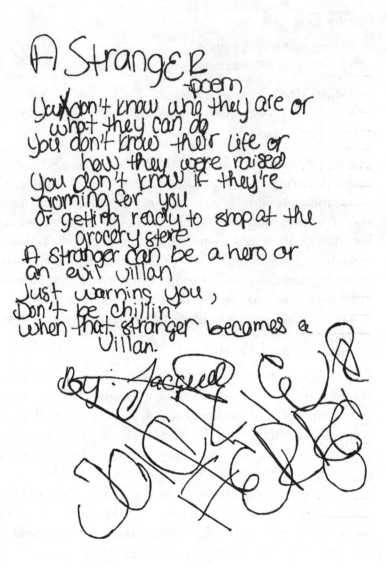

Figure 1-1

You don't know who they are or what they can do
You don't know their life or how they were raised
You don't know if they're coming for you
Or getting ready to shop at the grocery store
A stranger can be a hero or an evil villain
Just warning you,
Don't be chillin'
When that stranger becomes a villain.

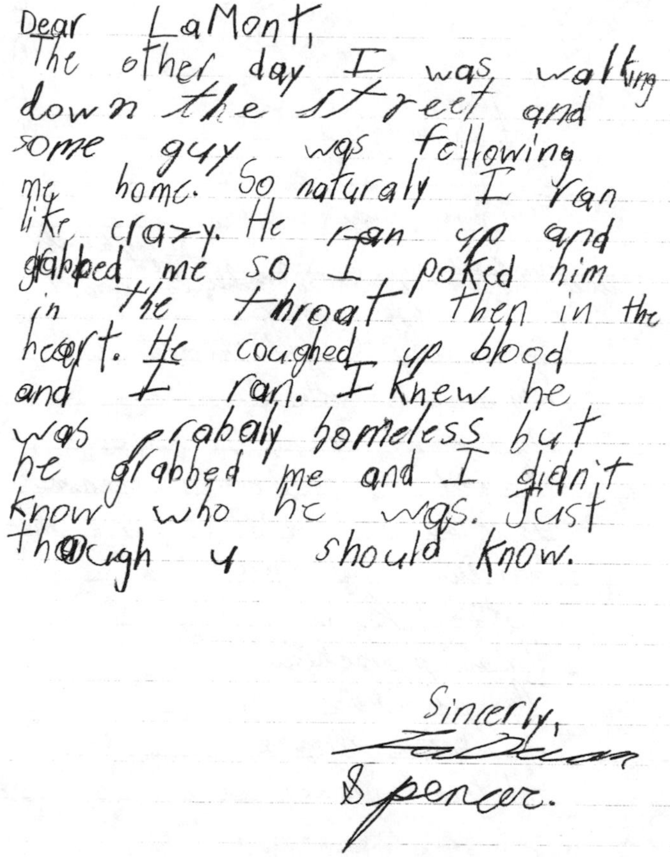

Dear LaMont,
The other day I was walking
down the street and
some guy was following
me home. So naturaly I ran
like crazy. He ran up and
grabbed me so I poked him
in the throat then in the
heart. He coughed up blood
and I ran. I knew he
was probaly homeless but
he grabbed me and I didn't
know who he was. Just
though u should know.

Sincerly,
Spencer.

Figure 1-2

Dear LaMont,

The other day I was walking
down the street and
some guy was following
me home. So naturally I ran
like crazy. He ran up and
grabbed me so I poked him
in the throat then in the
heart. He coughed up blood
and I ran. I knew he
was probably homeless but
he grabbed me and I didn't
know who he was. Just
thought you should know.

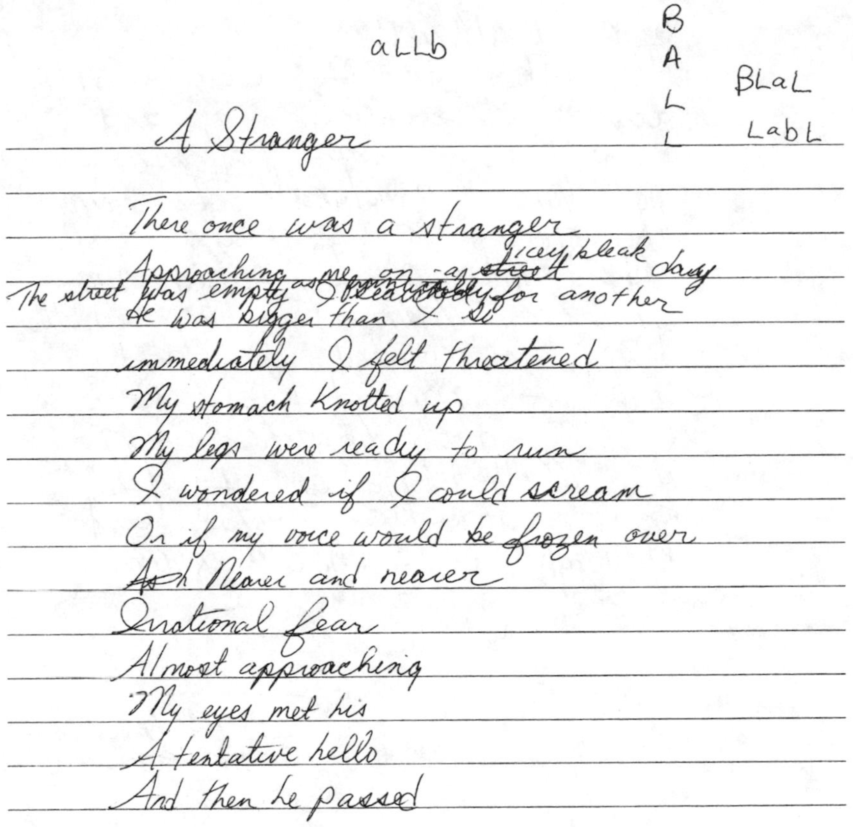

aLLb

B
A
L
L

BLaL

LabL

A Stranger

There once was a stranger
Approaching me on an ~~street~~ icy bleak day
The street was empty as I frantically searched for another
He was bigger than I so
immediately I felt threatened
My stomach knotted up
My legs were ready to run
I wondered if I could scream
Or if my voice would be frozen over
~~And~~ Nearer and nearer
Irrational fear
Almost approaching
My eyes met his
A tentative hello
And then he passed

Figure 1-3

There once was a stranger
Approaching me on an icy bleak day
The street was empty as I frantically searched for another
He was bigger than I so immediately I felt threatened
My stomach knotted up
My legs were ready to run
I wondered if I could scream
Or if my voice would be frozen over
Nearer and nearer
Irrational fear
Almost approaching
My eyes met his
A tentative hello
And then he passed.

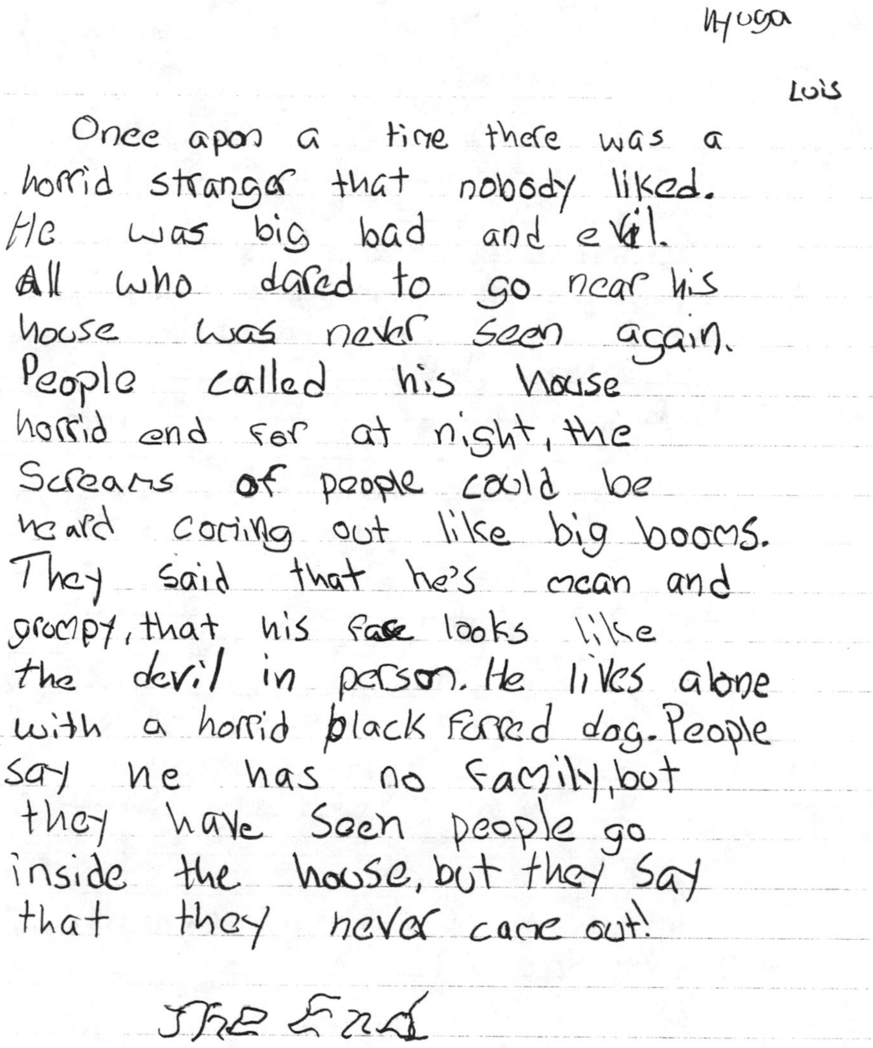

Hyuga

Luis

Once upon a time there was a
horrid stranger that nobody liked.
He was big bad and evil.
All who dared to go near his
house was never seen again.
People called his house
horrid end for at night, the
Screams of people could be
heard coming out like big booms.
They said that he's mean and
grompy, that his face looks like
the devil in person. He lives alone
with a horrid black furred dog. People
say he has no family, but
they have Seen people go
inside the house, but they say
that they never came out!

The End

Figure 1-4

Once upon a time there was a horrid stranger that nobody liked. He was big
bad and evil. All who dared to go near his house was never seen again. People
called his house Horrid End for at night, the screams of people could be heard
coming out like big booms. They said that he's mean and grumpy, that his face
looks like the devil in person. He lives alone with a horrid black furred dog.
People say he has no family, but they have seen people go inside the house,
but they say that they never came out!
The End

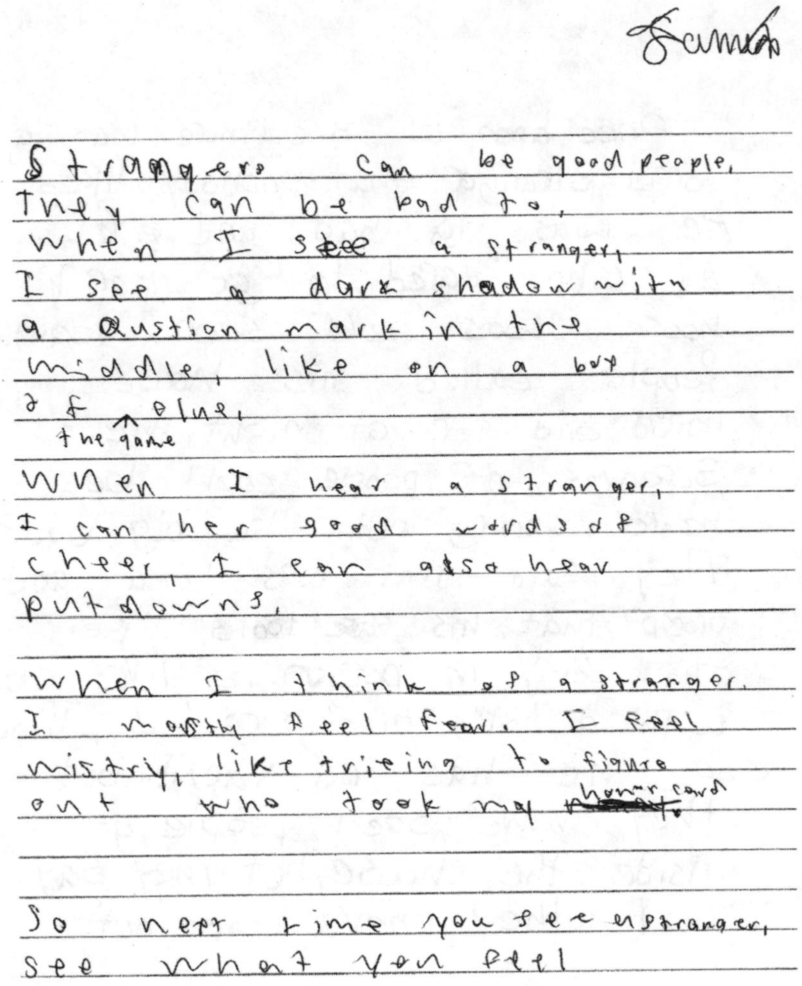

[Handwritten student text:]

Strangers can be good people.
They can be bad to.
When I see a stranger,
I see a dark shadow with
a Qustion mark in the
middle, like on a box
of Clue.
the game

When I hear a stranger,
I can her good words of
cheer, I can also hear
put downs.

When I think of a stranger.
I mostly feel fear. I feel
mistry, like trieing to figure
out who took my money card.

So next time you see a stranger,
see what you feel

Figure 1-5

Strangers can be good people. They can be bad too. When I see a stranger, I see a dark shadow with a question mark in the middle, like on a box of the game Clue.

When I hear a stranger, I can hear good words of cheer. I can also hear put-downs.

When I think of a stranger, I mostly feel fear. I feel mystery, like trying to figure out who took my money card.

So next time you see a stranger, see what you feel.

What kinds of things about life, culture, and writing are the No Names teaching one another? Rather than going for the gore, they express basic truths of the human condition: life can be scary, unpredictable, not what it seems. On some level we are all strangers and, paradoxically, that's something that connects us ("You don't know if they're coming for you or getting ready to shop at the grocery store"). Each draft is strikingly individual in voice, style, and point of view. The range of genre surprises and delights: fiction, nonfiction, poem, modern fable, letter, fairy tale/horror/satire ("*THE END*"), personal narrative bordering on allegory ("a dark shadow with a question mark in the middle"). Point of view? Name it and it's here: past, present, future; first person, second person, third person; omniscient and limited. Rhythm, rhyme, and the wondrous play of language ("Don't be chillin'/When that stranger becomes a villain"). Truth, image, symbol, and telling detail are here. Engaging audience through surprise, suspense, and direct address are here. Writing often tends to be taught in discrete elements: "Today we'll learn about images." In their writing circle, the No Names teach one another through the decisions they make about their writing. Because they are all exploring the same topic, the decisions become more clearly defined. They may have No Names, but they are all writers engaging one another, learning from one another.

Many adults belong to writing groups of one kind or another. Because they want to become better writers, they eagerly join, participate, and search for new members. They rearrange their lives so they have time to write and meet with other writers to share and respond to writing. Most professional writers share drafts with a small circle of family and friends as well. It's what might be termed an "authentic" process. As we look for lessons we can learn about how writing works in the everyday world of adults and professional writers, the classroom potential for writing circles seems largely unexplored and underutilized. This is what writers do. They write and share writing and integrate response.

If we are interested in infusing authentic real-world writing experiences into our classrooms, writing circles stand ready to help us do so. Like adults in their writing groups, kids in writing circles learn from one another and form a community of writers. Instead of one teacher of writing for thirty kids, there are thirty teachers of writing plus one! Every student does have something to learn about writing from every other student, as reader and writer. Through writing circles, every kid is a writer, every kid is a teacher of writing.

Democracy Now

Writing circles democratize the classroom by demystifying writing and creating an environment in which:

- Kids work to help one another become stronger writers.
- Every kid can be a successful writer, has a say in topic selection, and is encouraged to write from his own point of view, her own point of view, in an individual voice.

It's a win-win in the all too prevalent no-win—no-win called "writing in school." Writing circles enhance the writing self-image—for everyone. At the core of writing circles is the belief that every student is a writer and an equal in the larger community of writers.

Further Exploration

Through writing circles, kids develop kernels or drafts that can go on to become polished pieces. Publishing is a standard step. After kids have written and shared numerous drafts, they choose all or part of one draft to develop, revise, edit, and take through the publishing circle (see Chapter 10). You'll see more enthusiasm from kids for what Lucy Calkins (1994) calls the "process of growing meaning" (24) because, in their writing circles, kids have selected their own topics, explored these topics in their own way, and received response from the other kids in the circle. When kids look back over their writing circle drafts to find a writing kernel to explore more fully through the publishing circle, they often find much to choose from. There is a classroom of kids, most eager—and all ready—to take their writing to the next step, motivated to develop, revise, and edit because their writing has been supported by their peers, clarified through the writing of other kids in their circle, and often encouraged through whole-class sharing. Writing circles are seed beds where writing ideas germinate and quality writing grows.

Differentiated Instruction

Wanted: writing instruction that engages every kid in my classroom. We all know that kids are at different places in their writing development, at different chapters in their unfolding writing histories. In terms of writing development and proficiency, no two kids are in the same place and there is a lot of distance between many. Writing circles welcome all kids at their level of writing ability, celebrate that writing, and help them take their skill to the next level:

> The students definitely like writing circles, and many wrote more than expected. I noticed that even my reluctant writers enjoyed it. The students were obviously excited on the days we participated in the circles. Sometimes a cheer would erupt when I announced that was the activity for the day.
> —Jane Borden

The goal is for each kid to write about the consensus topic in the best way they can. It's like a sketch instead of the oil portrait framed in gold leaf on the wall. As artists have demonstrated, sketching leads to vision and craft. The same holds true for kids' drafts. Because what they write is their decision, writing circles invite and support all the kids in the classroom—where they are as well as where they are going.

Writing Confidence

There is abundant evidence that kids' attitudes toward writing are significant factors in their becoming better writers. Studying the writing experiences, attitudes, and achievement of first through sixth graders, Ruth Knudson (1995) found that, even after factoring in grade level, attitudes toward writing predicted writing achievement. Albert Bandura (1982) maintains that children's self-perception of writing ability is a decisive factor in their subsequent writing growth.

Key to kids' becoming better writers is how they feel about writing and themselves as writers. If kids don't see themselves as writers, it's difficult for them to become stronger writers. If kids dislike writing, the path to full authorship will wash out in front of them. The writing wounded. There they are in every classroom. Kids who, for whatever reason, dislike writing and see it as an adversary. Kids with no confidence in themselves as writers. Many of the writing wounded have been injured by linking writing and grades. How many of our students have more negative than positive experiences with writing? Writing circles embrace and rehabilitate the writing wounded while continuing to challenge the more confident and experienced writers in the class.

At Milwaukee's Tippecanoe School, fourth, fifth, sixth, and seventh graders worked in writing circles through the fall and spring of 2006. Kids were asked how confident they were about their writing before beginning their writing circle experiences and again afterward. The results, reported by Tippecanoe's literacy coach, Deborah Zaffiro, are presented in Figure 1-6.

Figure 1-6

Changes in Student Confidence in Writing

	Percent of Students Confident About Writing Prior to Circles	Percent of Students Confident About Writing Since Being Involved in Circles	Percent of Change
Fourth Grade	43%	67%	+24%
Fifth Grade	36%	50%	+14%
Sixth Grade	28%	71%	+43%
Seventh Grade	29%	59%	+30%

Does feeling more confident about writing necessarily make for a better writer? The answer is a resounding *yes*. Research and common sense tell us that kids' self-perception of their writing ability significantly affects their writing achievement. As one student commented, "Writing circles are really fun! We get to talk about our feelings, write about what we want. You're not judged or ridiculed."

Ever wish there was a structure that lets kids work collaboratively to generate writing topics, complete drafts, learn and practice positive ways of response, and develop published pieces? A structure that allows kids to retain ownership of the process while working together to help one another become better writers? A way that challenges confident writers and encourages struggling writers? A dynamic through which every kid in the class can have a feeling of success, a sense of what it means to be a writer? Writing circles are here to grant those wishes.

Welcome.

The Good, The Bad get down to work.

For the past two weeks I've been using writing circles in my classroom every morning during our writer's workshop. The second graders love it. They came up with their own names: Three Amigos, Thinking Hards, Ice Cream Team, Lord of the Rings, Snakes, and Anacondas. I made packets for the children to start out with—the first page is a list of writing genres. They have been choosing [topics] from the list but have also been inspired to choose topics as they hear other groups share their writing. Basically, they choose a genre and a topic and hear other circles share their writing. They write for about fifteen minutes. They share in their circles and choose someone to share with the whole class. When everyone is ready to share, one person from each group shares with the whole group—I encourage children to make comments or ask questions. After the whole-group share, the circles go back to work and choose a topic for the next day and write it down. Some continue the topic they were writing on, especially if it's fiction and they have a good story going. We share what each group will be writing about for the next day. I would say we spend forty-five minutes to one hour before lunch each day. They're very disappointed when the time is over.

—Jennifer McDonell

The Basics

Isolating the basic structure of writing circles belies the interdependent, recursive nature of the approach. The art of teaching depends on adequately preparing students so they can be successful, anticipating potential problems, and having the openness to adapt (and take advantage of) the unexpected. That being said, writing circles do have a number of distinct features.

Thirteen Steps to Quality Writing

1. *Groups name their writing circle and choose a common topic.* Groups of four to six kids work well. Groups are usually heterogeneous with kids of mixed abilities. (Strategies for grouping kids are described in Chapter 3 on pages 36–38.) When writing circle teachers get together, they inevitably entertain each other with the creative names kids give their groups: The Good The Bad, The Sloths, Remember Us, Four Amigos, Soldier Boyz, Peanut Butter Jellies, The Cupid Shuffle, TWGWARLN (The Writing Group with a Really Long Name). Kids naming their writing circle is more than a sure-fire ice breaker. Choosing a good name provides a positive experience in collaborative decision making; the name also gives the respective circle members identity and a sense of ownership.

2. *Kids write on the chosen topic, using any point of view or genre.* At the center of writing circles is kids' writing. Kids create a draft (using pencils, pens, or laptops) on the topic they have agreed on as a group. Kids basically write about the topic in any way they think will be effective. The amount of time spent writing varies from grade to grade, classroom to classroom, from Donald Graves' (1985) "ten-minute writes" to twenty or thirty minutes. The focus is on what kids want to say instead of conventions like spelling, punctuation, and grammar. Some kids will spend more time on

their drafts than others. Some will revise, some won't; some will write a lot, and some will still be working on that. The bottom line is kids write what they want to write the way they want to write it. For this to happen, the teacher has to be ready to hand over some control. It's worth doing. In its place is an increased sense of kids' pride of writing ownership. (If you're worrying about kids not being able to draft fluently, consider some of the strategies found in Chapter 5.)

3. *Writing circle minilessons focus on management and craft.* The first five or ten minutes of class before the writing circles meet usually consist of a minilesson focused on small-group collaboration, writing craft, ways of responding. Anything needed to support writing circles and kids' writing. Initially, the teacher presents the minilesson. Once writing circles are up and running, minilessons can also be presented by individual kids and selected writing circles. Minilessons are all about timing, and they need to be brief enough to be called upon at the "teachable moment." Frequently, this moment occurs right before kids meet in their writing circles—especially if the focus of the minilesson is on how kids respond to each other's writing. Other minilessons concern management and craft: how to make the writing circles function more smoothly and how to become a stronger writer (see Chapter 7).

4. *Writing circles meet.* How often and for how long writing circles meet varies. Writing can be done in school, at home, or both. In some classrooms, writing circles are part of writing workshop. In other classrooms, writing circles meet separately once a week, twice a week, or every day. Generally, writing circles continue for three to five weeks; the publication circle requires at least an additional week.

Writing circles do not take the place of writing workshop; they are a companion activity, and fit easily into the writing workshop framework and time period. In many classrooms, writing circles alternate with writing workshop—kids meet in writing circles one day and then draft and revise during the next day's writing workshop.

Within the circles, kids take on certain responsibilities to keep the group moving forward. Your class may use different terminology, but two key roles are "timekeeper" and "first writer." These roles rotate with each writing circle meeting. Knowing who is going to share their writing first ("first writer") helps jump-start the circles. The "timekeeper" has to do a little math (amount of sharing time divided by number of kids) to ensure each writer has a chance to share some writing and receive responses.

5. *Kids share their writing.* When kids join their writing circle, they bring along their draft on the topic previously chosen by their circle. During the meeting, kids read their drafts to the other kids in their circle. Reading aloud keeps the focus on what the writer has to say instead of errors in transcription and correctness. As one student remarked, "Writing circles made me a better writer because it helped me read my writing in front of my peers. I like hearing other people's writing pieces. It made me enjoy writing at school because that way it was easier to get work done."

6. *Kids respond to one another's writing.* In writing circles, kids practice and experience responding constructively to writing, in structured, affirmative ways. Kids listen to each other's drafts, knowing what to listen for—thanks to teacher-led minilessons. We need to teach kids positive ways to talk to one another about their writing. When peer response becomes a series of "that's good" statements, it's largely because kids haven't learned other, more specific and positive ways to talk about writing.

   It's often the writer who specifies the kind of response they want. Writing circles exist to support and inform the writer, and what the writer needs often determines the type of response they receive from the other kids in the group. The writer knows what kind of response to request because many ways of responding have been modeled and defined during earlier demonstration minilessons. In writing circles, the purpose of response is to affirm the writer and honor the writing.

7. *Each circle chooses their next topic.* Choosing a new topic inevitably sparks another good discussion, with the final decision reached through consensus. To put it as a double negative: no kid should write about a topic they have no interest in. In order to expedite choosing a new topic, each kid brings at least one new topic

suggestion to every circle meeting. Kids who have been supported in listing and discovering new writing ideas will have numerous promising topics to choose from (see Chapters 5 and 7). Writing circles sometimes appropriate another circle's topic, which is just another earmark of a generous collaborative community.

Kids go around the circle, each member proposing a new writing idea. Sometimes there's quick agreement; sometimes a couple of suggestions attract interest until one is revised, added to, refined, and chosen. Occasionally, none of the proposed topics hold real interest. When that happens kids generally have little trouble using the proposed topics to get to a more exciting one. Often, all it takes is for someone to ask, "How would you write about that?" A circle that repeatedly has difficulty deciding on their next writing topic is ready for a strategic topic search conference.

Student: "I like being able to choose topics with a group, because if you gave us topics and if we didn't like them we would be less inclined to do it."

8. *Each writing circle shares their new topic and some of the current day's writing with the whole class.* It's a good idea to hold off sharing drafts with the whole class until kids feel comfortable within their groups. But it is vital to share new topics from each group from the first meeting on. As each circle announces their new topic to the rest of the class, many kids start to make a mental note on how they would write about "that one." Sudden flashes of premeditation *about* writing. Kids starting to think like writers.

When circles do begin to share some of their writing with the whole class, it's writing that has already been shared and supported in the smaller writing circles, so there is little anxiety and a lot of excitement. This is usually a brief, one- or two-minute glimpse—a writing window—into each writing circle.

There are many ways circles can share their writing. Sometimes the circle members decide how they are going to do this; sometimes sharing grows out of the kind of response kids have just given one another's writing. For example, if minilessons have been focusing on the importance of concrete details in writing, kids in each circle might be asked to respond to each other's writing by pointing out details that were particularly effective. For whole-class sharing, each circle is then asked to share "the best of" list of concrete details from their circle writings. A favorite kind of sharing is for each circle to "nominate" someone to read all or part of their writing to the class. We don't, however, want the same kids sharing their writing every time. If this starts to happen, we use strategies that showcase a small part of each kid's writing (see Chapter 9).

9. *Kids reflect on what happened in the writing circle and take notes in their notebook.* At the end of each writing circle meeting, kids spend two or three minutes jotting down their thoughts. Sometimes, this "think-back" is guided by the teacher. Generally, it is self-directed as kids jot down their observations about the day's writing circle experience: what they are learning about writing, how well the writing circles are going, what they think about the writing of other kids in their circle, what they found of interest today. Ideally, this reflection is an opportunity for kids to understand what they are learning about writing as individual writers and group members. Kids also record the day's circle topic, type of response, new topic, and their responsibilities for the next meeting. A think-back reflection template is provided in Figure 2-1.

10. *Periodically, kids review their rough pieces and select the most promising one.* Kids' writing circle drafts contain many promising "starts" or kernels for finished pieces. Once kids have seven or eight drafts (enough to provide a number of promising options), they review their work and choose a draft, part of a draft, or an idea they want to think and write more about.

11. *Writers collaboratively revise, polish, and publish their writing.* At this point, the writing circle becomes a publishing circle: kids help one another develop their chosen pieces of writing and bring them to publication. Since kids are already comfortable with their writing and comfortable working with one another, the transition from writing circle to publishing circle is smooth and natural.

12. *Circle members serve as one another's agents, illustrators, reviewers, and editors.* Taking on roles from the publishing world (but not the competitiveness), kids look at one another's writing as specialists. As *agents*, kids advocate for one another's writing; as *illustrators* they encourage one another to think about the presentation and

Writing Circle Think-Back

Date: Name: Writing circle name:

Writing topic:

Type of response:

Draft ready?   Yes/No

Did I share my writing with the whole class? Yes/No

My suggestion for today's new writing topic:

New writing topic chosen by my writing circle:

Reflection on today's writing circle:

For the *next* writing circle meeting, I am:

   First Writer: Yes/No   Timekeeper: Yes/No

Don't forget to bring a new writing topic suggestion to the next writing circle.

Writing Circles by Jim Vopat (Heinemann: Portsmouth, NH); © 2009 visual aspects of their writing; as *reviewers* they suggest revisions; as *editors* they proofread one another's work and focus on issues of correctness and final presentation. Then, as *authors* they complete their piece using the input and support of their publishing circle. By taking on each role, kids think about their writing in informative and insightful ways.

13. *Finished works are shared and celebrated publicly.* Every kid is an author. Final pieces are celebrated and published—displayed, read aloud, posted online, collected into booklets, and distributed. Kids reflect on the full range of their writing circle work and write a final "think-back" on what they have learned about themselves as writers and group members. Kids review the contents of their writing circle notebook and document their "good faith" effort (see Chapter 11).

Sharing drafts in the circle.

FAQ's

What about kids who don't have topics to write about or aren't able to draft fluently?

When kids join writing circles, they need to be ready with a list of topics that they want to write about and feel comfortable drafting. In other words, we need to spend time in advance helping kids identify good topics and demonstrating and giving kids practice in quick extended drafting. There are, to borrow Stephanie Harvey's phrase, many "strategies that work." Chapter 3 includes suggestions for getting kids ready to write.

How many kids make a circle?

Writing circles usually number between three and six kids. As with literature circles, we want to form small, functional groups—not so large that sharing and response will become rushed, and not so small that the group will find it hard to function if one of the kids is absent. Circles of four or five kids are common. This ensures a variety of kinds of writing and points of view. Each circle doesn't have to have the same number of kids.

How often are writing circles scheduled? Once a week over the entire term? Every day for three or four weeks, or for a few months alternating with writing workshop?

Writing circles are scheduled so kids can count on them. A recurrent, consistent, dependable schedule allows kids to plan their writing. If you've scheduled writing circles for every Tuesday and Thursday and you miss a Tuesday, be prepared for some disappointed kids. Such disappointment is not the best way to measure success, but it indicates how a recurrent, predictable schedule helps to motivate kids. We want kids to look forward to writing circles, and consistent scheduling (in terms of day and time) helps make that happen.

At the primary level, teachers often divide writing circle sessions into writing time and sharing time. At the end of sharing time, kids come to consensus about their new writing topic and write a brief reflection. For example:

Monday	Tuesday	Wednesday	Thursday	Friday
10:15–10:30 Write	10:15–10:30 Write	10:15–10:30 Write	10:15–10:30 Write	10:15–10:30 Write
10:30–11:00 Circles Meet	10:30–11:00 Circles Meet	10:30–11:00 Circles Meet	10:30–11:00 Circles Meet	10:30–11:00 Circles Meet

In self-contained classrooms, writing circles often alternate with writing workshop:

Monday	Tuesday	Wednesday	Thursday	Friday
10:15–11:00 Circles Meet	10:15–11:00 Writing Workshop	10:15–11:00 Circles Meet	10:15–11:00 Writing Workshop	10:15–11:00 Circles Meet

Time gets tight in middle schools, where language arts are often assigned a double-period block:

Monday	Tuesday	Wednesday	Thursday	Friday
8:15–9:00 English	8:15–9:00 English	8:15–9:00 English	8:15–9:00 English	8:15–9:00 English
9:00–9:45 Circles Meet	9:00–9:45 Write	9:00–9:45 Circles Meet	9:00–9:45 Write	9:00–9:45 Circles Meet

Time constraints are even tighter in high school:

Monday	Tuesday	Wednesday	Thursday	Friday
8:15–9:00 English	8:15–9:00 English	8:15–9:00 English	8:15–9:00 English	8:15–9:00 Writing Circle

In order for a once-a-week writing circle like this to work, prior class time would need to be set aside for training—consecutive days spent modeling the process, helping kids generate writing topic lists, and generally becoming familiar with the writing circle structure and expectations.

How about the timing of the writing circle itself?

In order to complete the various writing circle activities—sharing, responding, selecting a new topic, and reflecting—kids need to have a clear sense of how much time is available for what. Generally, writing circles take between thirty-five and forty-five minutes (sometimes less in the early primary grades), depending on the way kids respond to one another's writing, how much time is allotted for new topic selection, and whether or not kids start a new draft immediately. A typical period might look like this:

Whole-class writing circle minilesson (5 minutes)
Kids sharing and responding to writing (15–20 minutes)
New topic selection (5 minutes)
Whole-class sharing (5–10 minutes)
Writing circle notebook reflection (3–5 minutes)
Writing time (if available)

Something that takes one group ten minutes can take another group thirteen minutes and still another group fifteen minutes. Keeping kids who are essentially "finished" on task while others are still working is one of the major challenges of group work. This isn't much of a problem in writing circles, however. A circle that finishes choosing a new topic early and has some time before the announced whole class sharing, for example, can either start their new writing or discuss ideas for how to write about the new topic. Discussing their thinking about the new topic invariably gives kids additional ideas and generates enthusiasm.

I'll admit it. I'm uncomfortable with all the uncorrected drafts.

It's important to keep in mind (and to remind kids) that they will be choosing a kernel from their drafts to develop, revise, edit, and polish through the publishing circle. Ironically, kids often tend to take the writing they share with their peers more seriously than the writing they produce for the teacher. Writing circles give kids a structure that allows them to relax and explore their writing in a supportive, collaborative environment. From these many drafts emerges the kind of writing kids *want* to inhabit and make better. The series of drafts ultimately motivates kids to take their writing to the next level. And because the drafting also connects many kids with the realities of writing voice and audience, it helps make them stronger writers. As Zemelman, Daniels, and Hyde observe in *Best Practice: New Standards for*

Teaching and Learning in America's Schools, "the best language-learning occurs when students attempt actual communication and then see how real listeners/readers react" (1999, 59).

How do I assess my students' work in writing circles?

There are a number of choices for assessing kids' work and giving them credit for writing circles (see Chapter 11). For this assessment to be fruitful, kids need to keep a writing circle notebook. The notebook can be a folder, a binder, or a stapled or bound booklet. The important thing is to provide a way for kids to keep track of their writing circle process—drafts, topics, response strategies, daily reflections, whether they were first writer or timekeeper. Standardized "thinking back" reflection sheets can be collected, quickly reviewed, and returned to kids, who then need to secure these sheets in their notebook. The writing circle notebook makes it possible for kids to review what they have accomplished and document their "good faith" effort.

Yes, "good faith" effort. It makes a lot of sense to reward effort in learning when the effort *is* the learning. The process of writing circles leads to better writing, and it is appropriate and just to award credit for full participation. Kids are basically engaged in writing circle work or they aren't, and it's their responsibility to show sufficient work in their writing circle notebook to make the case for such good faith effort. If necessary, effort easily translates into a grade. If kids complete the writing circle assignments they get a B; if they've done a good job they get an A; if their efforts have been less than good, the grade is lowered proportionately. ("Good faith" effort is more fully explained in Chapter 11.)

How much time should students be given to write?

Some teachers set a minimum requirement—ten minutes per draft, for example—that becomes longer in the higher grades. In classrooms where kids create their circle drafts during writing workshop, the amount of time spent on them is substantially longer. In general, though, this consideration has more to do with taking the time necessary to explore the agreed-on topic. Drafts usually become longer and more fully developed with more practice writing and hearing writing read aloud. Some kids can get stuck in writing drafts too brief to explore or really begin to develop their writing idea. Through modeling and minilessons we talk and demonstrate what it means to draft enough to discover meaning as opposed to writing so little as to shut the door on discovery. Basically, the audience expectations established by the writing circle structure preclude the "amount of student writing" issue. When kids see that they are writing for one another and listen to and enjoy the longer, more thoughtful drafts of their peers, they invariably put more time and thought into their work.

How do you form groups? How do you keep track of what each circle is doing? Does the teacher join a circle? How do kids reach a consensus? What do kids write? What about genres? When . . . .

The more answers, the more questions: teaching and learning as inquiry. Not to worry. The practice of writing circles itself clarifies these questions and provides a series of answers. Teachers find their own answers when they believe the process benefits kids. Teachers who believe in something find ways to make it work. Answers often present themselves once writing circles are underway—are revealed in the process. In his poem "The Love Song of J. Alfred Prufrock," T. S. Eliot writes, "Oh, do not ask what is it?/Let us go and make our visit."

In the chapters ahead are strategies to motivate kids to write and discover topics that interest them; minilessons on management and writing craft; activities to build community and a spirit of collaboration; writing circle schedules; publication role sheets; discussions of the writing circle notebook and how writing circles become publishing circles; constructive friendly ways for kids to respond to one another's writing; ways of sharing and celebrating writing as a whole class; and assessment suggestions.

But first, ready for day one?

Getting Started

Writing circle success depends on kids feeling comfortable—comfortable drafting, comfortable sharing their writing, comfortable receiving response from other kids, comfortable working together. But many kids aren't that comfortable participating in independent small-group work or writing fluent drafts. Chapters 4 and 5 describe and explore community building and writing strategies that make classroom conditions propitious. We can always do more community building, learn more group process, build more writing confidence, and generate more writing ideas. Some classrooms need more work in these areas than others.

However, when kids generally feel comfortable with each other and writing, the time is ripe for writing circles. Each of us will know when our class is ready.

Day One

In anticipation of day one, you'll want to figure out how writing circles fit into the classroom schedule. Eight or more writing circle meetings are a good number to initially plan for. Whether these writing circle meetings occur within a four- to six-week period or longer depends on the individual classroom. If kids are going to choose a kernel from their rough drafts to revise and edit in a publishing circle, make time for a minimum of five additional meetings.

Before taking the plunge, check to make sure everyone has his or her swimwear on, so to speak. Tell kids in advance what writing circles are and how being in writing circles will help them become stronger writers. Give kids a sense of the "why" of writing circles—kids working together to help one another become better writers. Do kids have a general understanding of how writing circles work—choosing a topic, writing, sharing, responding, and reflecting? Writing circle notebooks and think-back reflection forms at the ready? (See Chapter 6.) Have kids got their writing idea/topic cards and other topic lists? (See the "Stack the Deck for Writing" discussion in Chapter 5.)

The first day of writing circles is different from the days that follow, since kids will not be coming to this first circle with drafts they have written. Dive in! The writing's fine.

Form Writing Circles

This seems simple enough. A principle of writing circles is all kids have something to teach one another, and that's also an argument for heterogeneous grouping. But there's a lot of variation in how writing circles form from classroom to classroom. You know best what kind of grouping is going to work for your students. There are wonderful writing circles in which kids choose one another, and wonderful writing circles where there was some teacher intervention in the formation process. The following are some ways to form heterogeneous mixed ability writing circles.

Count Off

The most basic way is to figure out how many writing circles you want and then have kids count off by that number. If you have a class of twenty-eight students and you think five writing circles each with five or six kids would be ideal, count off in fives. Then, send them off: "All the ones in a circle by the windows, all the twos over by the door," and so on.

Choose a Color

Put together a pack of different-color index cards—one color for each circle, one card for each kid in the class. If you have a class of twenty-eight kids and want six circles, you will have twenty-eight cards in six colors, two groups of four (in red and purple, for example) and four groups of five (blue, green, yellow, and orange, for example). Shuffle the cards and let kids pick one (choice) or simply deal them out (chance). Kids with red cards form one circle; kids with blue cards another. "The yellow group meets out in the hall."

Pass the Hat

Decide the number of groups you want, then prepare slips of paper numbered one through that number until you have as many slips of paper as there are kids in the class. Put the slips of paper in a hat or small box and have every kid draw one. As with counting off, the number they draw determines their writing circle. Much more open to chance when the hat is first passed; definitely "fate" toward the end.

What Sign Are You?

My horoscope says that at some point there will be scientific studies and Ph.D. dissertations about how a writer's astrological sign affects their writing. Until then, grouping kids by astrological sign remains simply adventurous. "Okay. Who's a Pisces? Born between February 20 and March 20. Says here that the more someone discourages you, the more determined you are to go ahead and do it. Let's see the hands—Pisces. Or is it fins?" Note the number of kids with each sign and share a part of their daily horoscope with them. Cancer: "Sometimes your laid-back attitude can tell against you in that others believe you are not really interested in what you are doing. Prove them wrong over the next twenty-four hours." Talk about horoscopes as a writing genre. Ask if kids think the daily horoscope is true or not. Then do the math—combining signs that only have a few kids—guided by the number of writing circles you think are optimal. If you want to skip the horoscope, just group by birthdays in the various months.

> Student: "I prefer choosing my group. I don't like not being able to pick my group. I also want longer sharing time. I like keeping the topics broad. It's a group decision."

Who Would Be in Your Dream Writing Circle?

Another way to form circles is to help kids pick who they want to be in their circle. This needs to be done before the first writing circle meeting. To avoid kids' inclinations to be swayed solely by friendship and popularity, have kids list five other kids who they think could really help them with writing—because of their different points of view, personalities, talents. Collect the lists and make the best matches you can. Explain to kids that they're not all going to get all their choices since that's mathematically impossible, but they'll end up with many of their choices.

The role of the teacher in this kind of student choice varies in each classroom. Chicago area high school teacher Nancy Steineke's description of how she helps kids select their literature circle groups gives a sense of the kind of teacher negotiation that can ultimately enhance the group dynamic at any grade level:

I try to tweak the groups for optimal success based on personality, discussion skill level, and homework habits. Gender and personality are also considerations. I also always try to make sure the kids are working with some new people, since one of my goals is for all of the students to meet and work with everyone else before the end of the year. All of these are individual judgment calls, but if you've been working with a class for a while you can usually make them pretty quickly. (2002, 136)

Choose a Topic

Once kids are in writing circles, put them to work by helping them reach consensus about their first writing circle topic. Chapter 5 offers many ways to help kids generate writing ideas. Here's one, a variation of the stack-the-topic-deck strategy described on page 71):

1. Each kid, in advance, has prepared three index cards, an idea for a writing topic written on each card. Encourage kids to include genres as possible writing ideas. "A Contemporary Fairy Tale" and "Friends" could be equally promising topics.
2. Once they are in their writing circles, kids mix the cards together and then redistribute them randomly so everyone still has three topic cards (but probably not their own or at least not all their own).
3. Each kid considers the three new topic cards and chooses one.
4. These final topic cards (one per kid) are then passed around the circle.
5. On each topic card, kids respond with a plus, a check, or a minus (or a star, a question mark, and an X)—some coding that basically says I like the topic; I'm okay with the topic; or, no way, the topic won't work for me.
6. After everyone has marked the topic cards, narrow the topics by throwing out any card with a "no way" indication.
7. A consensus topic may have already emerged from the remaining cards, or there might be two topics that spark interest.
8. Give each circle enough time to discuss the most popular topics and choose one they all want to write about.
9. Encourage kids to share ideas they have for how they will write about their chosen topic: different points of view, different genres.

Name Your Writing Circle

After they've chosen their topic, kids name their writing circle. These names are invariably witty and outrageous—the source of much amusement and delight. Flying Penguins, Trapped in School, Skateboarding Black Cats, Hippie Gnomes, The People People, Headless Cupids, The Sloths, Remember Us, Germs. The names are memorable because they usually exemplify a clever use of language. An earnest attempt to define and engage through writing. What a difference a name makes. Naming their circle gives kids a sense of ownership and demonstrates the creative synergy of working together. If kids can't decide on a good name, they can temporarily call themselves In Progress or The Yet Unnamed (an actual adult writing group) or something else that's tentative until the right name emerges. Circles can always rename themselves as their identity becomes more clearly defined.

Identify First Writer and Timekeeper

The first writer will start the next writing circle by reading their draft aloud. The timekeeper makes sure that sharing and topic selection happen on schedule. First writer and timekeeper responsibilities rotate from meeting to meeting. Who will be first writer and timekeeper is decided during the *prior* writing circle so kids know in advance what their responsibilities will be. That way, when writing circles meet, there is little delay in the start of sharing, and all the steps in the process are guaranteed to take place. A quick means of accountability is to have each timekeeper jot down the basic information on a form (see Figure 3-1) and give it to the teacher at the end of each writing circle meeting.

Figure 3-1. At Our Next Writing Circle

Circle name

New topic

First writer   Timekeeper

                      (name)   (name)

Share Names and Topics with the Whole Class

A spokesperson from each circle states their chosen name and writing topic. (If kids hear a topic from another circle that appeals to them, they can write it down and choose it themselves later.) Have a brief class discussion about the range of writing topics that have been chosen. This is an opportunity for a minilesson on genres. Reiterate that kids can respond to their topic in the way they think will work best. Genre, point of view, concept, language, length, are all decisions made by the writer. If you plan to join a writing circle the next time they meet, note that topic so you can come prepared with your own draft. Emphasize that responses are *drafts* instead of thoroughly revised and edited final copies. That doesn't mean that kids don't or can't revise their draft, but it's not required.

Write

Kids begin writing about their topic. Whether they finish the draft outside class or have enough time to complete it in class (during writing workshop, for example) will be individual to your classroom. Just make sure everyone has a good start—do whatever it takes so kids have a draft to share when their writing circle meets next. Write a draft yourself as well, modeling the work of a more experienced writer. Pick the topic that appeals to you or the topic of the group you're planning to join.

Try a Think-Back Reflection

Five minutes or so before the end of the session, introduce kids to the record keeping and reflection process by having them complete their first writing circle "think-back" in their writing circle notebook. First, brainstorm some ideas about what this reflection might include. How did they feel about the process? Are they looking forward to working in writing circles? What are some ideas they have about their writing circle topic? What could they do differently next time? A standardized form (see Figure 2-1, p. 28) expedites the reflection, and should be kept in each kid's writing circle notebook, one for each writing circle meeting. (For the first writing circle, the reflection is abbreviated as shown in Figure 3-2.)

Remind kids to bring three things to the next writing circle meeting: (1) their writing circle notebook, (2) a completed draft response to their first writing circle topic, and (3) a new topic suggestion.

Writing Circle Think-Back (abbreviated for first meeting)

Date: Name: Writing circle name:

Reflection on today's writing circle:

For the *next* writing circle meeting, I am:

First writer   Yes/No   Timekeeper Yes/No

Don't forget to bring a new writing topic suggestion to the next writing circle.

Day Two: Up to Speed

As with many learning activities, once kids experience writing circles, they become more natural and relaxed (in the sense of knowing what happens when). But the process is still as surprising and unique as the writing created in each circle. In the second meeting (and subsequent ones), the recurrent writing circle structure becomes fully operational.

Minilesson

Kids will be sharing their first drafts in their writing circles today, so it's a good idea to frame the kind of response they'll give one another. Explain that one of the advantages of writing circles is that they offer a chance to learn and practice different ways of responding to one another's writing. "Today's response will be to tell the writer one thing you like about their writing. It can be something about what they say or how they wrote about the topic—something that will make the writer feel good about writing and sharing. No negative comments." Model this response by asking kids to jot down things that get their positive attention as you read a draft aloud. Here are some of the responses kids had after listening to their teacher read a draft about her favorite pet.

- "I could picture what you were saying."
- "You used a ton of descriptive words."
- "You used a simile and a couple of metaphors."
- "I could tell you really love your dog."
- "There were some well-worded sentences."

Ask kids to remind themselves of today's way of responding by writing *something positive* in the response section on the day's writing circle reflection form.

Kids Form Writing Circles

Help circles find locations that will be comfortable—far enough away from other circles so that everyone in the circle can hear one another. Encourage kids to literally sit in a circle facing each other. Check to make sure each circle has a first writer and timekeeper and that these kids know what their responsibilities are. Clarify ("attention timekeepers!") how much time is available for sharing, response, and new topic selection. Timekeepers must

divide the sharing and response time into equal units. After everyone is settled, first writers start right in, reading their draft.

Join a Circle

After checking that all the circles are up and running, join the one you
identified earlier, your own draft in hand ready to share. In each circle, kids
take turns sharing their drafts and listening to the other kids' responses.
Responses finished, kids share their predetermined new writing topics and
decide by consensus what to write about for the next meeting. The timekeeper's responsibility is to keep things moving along so circles finish on
time. If they finish early, kids can discuss ideas they have for how to write
about the newly chosen topic. Before time's up, kids in each circle also
need to decide who's going to be next meeting's timekeeper and first writer.
If there's still time left over, they can start writing.

Whole-Class Sharing

By now things have probably taken longer than you thought; it's definitely
time to bring the writing circles together as a whole class. Ask each writing

The teacher joins the circle.

circle to provide two basic points of information: (1) the name of their circle and (2) their new writing topic. Discuss the variety of topics and open up one or two by asking kids what ideas they have for how to write about them.

Think-Back Reflection

Kids will have a lot to say. This is the first time they have heard one another's writing. Help frame the response by asking kids to think of one thing they heard that they want to remember. Using a standardized form solves many future management issues: see the filled-in example in Figure 3-3.

Figure 3-3. Writing Circle Think-Back

Date: **11/3**   Writing circle name: **The Good, the Bad**
Writing topic: **Pets**

Name: **Jason P.**   Type of response: **Something positive**

Draft ready? (**Yes**)/No

Did I share my writing with the whole class? Yes/(**No**)

My suggestion for today's new writing topic: **Skateboarding**

New writing topic chosen by my writing circle: **Rotten food**

Reflection on today's writing circle: **It was fun to hear the stories. I feel sad about Mike's dog being hit by the car and that the vet had her put down.**

For the *next* writing circle meeting, I am:

First writer   (**Yes**)/No   Timekeeper Yes/(**No**)

Don't forget to bring a new writing topic suggestion to the next writing circle.

Do your own think-back reflection as well, jotting down something you learned or noticed about each kid in the writing circle you joined, something that sticks with you. If you can't recall anything, note that as well. (There is a sample anecdotal record sheet in Chapter 11.)

Caution: Process Ahead!

Writing circles never happen the same way or exactly how you think they will. That's a good thing. It means you and your students are part of an authentic process. As writing circles continue, learn from your own experience, encourage kids to share how they feel things are going, and provide opportunities for kids to suggest how to make circles work even better. Confer with kids who seem to be struggling. Anticipate possible difficulties and invite kids to help solve problems.

By the third or fourth writing circle meeting, it's time to give guidelines for how circles can share some of their writing with the whole class. "Today we're going to start sharing writing from each circle when we get together again as a whole class. Let's do nominations. Each circle nominates someone from their group to read all or part of their draft to us. Nominate kids whose writing you think we all should hear." Kids truly like listening to one another's writing—especially when enjoyment rather than judgment is the objective. Remind kids these are just drafts. The idea is low-risk whole-class sharing of writing, low on judgment, high on appreciation. (Chapter 9 suggests ten nonthreatening ways kids can share their writing with the whole class.) Some nominees may be nervous about reading to the whole class, but they have their writing circle to support them. Some circles decide to stand with and around their nominee as the person reads; at times a group member might volunteer to read the piece aloud on behalf of the reticent author.

Hearing your own words come alive in front of a large group definitely builds the confidence of emerging writers. When a nominee finishes reading their draft aloud, model a positive nonjudgmental responses yourself. Thank nominees for the experience ("Thanks, Taylor, I'll never think about robots in the same way again"), and if there's a detail in the writing you remember, say so. This is an opportunity to point out strong individual "voice." Make your response brief and to the point. After all the circle nominees have shared their draft, go around once again and have each circle state their new writing topic. Decide which writing circle you want to join the next time and note the topic, so you can be ready with your own draft.

Soon kids will be well into the essential writing circle rhythm of selecting a topic, writing, sharing, responding, and reflecting. In the swim of things.

What's the Teacher Doing?

There's a lot going on in the classroom during writing circles. To an outsider it might look as if you are just kicking back and enjoying yourself as the kids write and talk about their writing. To an extent, this is true. You certainly want to enjoy the experience, but you also are part of the process and actively collaborating. Through forethought and preparation, barely controlled chaos is transformed into the art of teaching. All the parts work in productive harmony.

Modeling

So what else is new? How we respond to learning does influence kids. Why not be intentional about it? In writing circles this means joining circles and sharing our writing. It means thinking aloud about the process, verbalizing our writing choices, and sharing our own reflections:

> I am really enjoying what we call "journal groups." Topics have been a lot more interesting than some of the things I would have dreamed up. My favorite part is taking part in the circles as a fellow writer. It is different than modeling for the whole class.
> —Jody Henderson-Sykes

The first few times writing circles meet, many teachers move from circle to circle to get a sense of how things are going and to help launch the circles successfully. Once circles are running smoothly, you can join a different circle each time. Be alert to which circles will benefit the most from your participation.

Select a circle in advance and have a draft ready to share on the day's topic. Share, respond, and help your circle reach consensus about the next writing idea. In addition to your writing, share your observations about how writing circles are going as well as how it feels to be part of the process. Think aloud about your writing choices, how it feels to be a writer, what kinds of decisions a writer makes, what you did to make the topic "one inch tall" your own. Keep your own writing circle notebook—your drafts, observations, anecdotal records, and reflections (described in Chapter 6). Select one of your drafts to revise and edit as part of the publishing circle. Teach from your own writing. Think aloud about your observations related to the social dynamics of writing circles, obviously tailoring your discussion to the age of your students. Talk to kids about reaching consensus, how it feels to respond, to work together—what helps the social dynamic and what could be improved.

When you join a writing circle you won't be first writer, because one of the members will have already assumed that responsibility. You also don't want to be "last writer" all the time. That's unnatural, and there's a teacher-is-the-final-word aspect to always reading last. Try to share your piece in the middle of the session. When it's time to select the new writing topic for the next writing circle meeting, help kids in the circle arrive at a consensus. (Since you probably won't join this same circle again next time, don't offer a writing topic of your own.)

The first time I shared, about dreams, I burst into tears. I didn't realize how powerful it was.
—Jane Borden

Orchestrating

- Set up the general guidelines for the writing circle—including time allocations: end time and how much time for writing (if in class), sharing in small groups, and selecting the next topic.
- Structure the way kids respond to one another's writing through minilessons, demonstrations, and fishbowl conferences. Follow up with practice in the writing circles. Kids need to understand how to respond to one another's writing. Once kids understand a variety of responses, they are ready for more ownership. As a circle, kids can decide on the specific response they will use—sometimes because it is a favorite, sometimes to practice something new. Most important, writers can specify the type of response they want. The more ways of responding kids understand, the more choices there are. Make the options clear. Kids need to know what to listen for as the writer shares a draft.
- Schedule time for each circle to share some writing and their next writing topic with the whole class. New writing ideas are always interesting and spark a lot of writer-like thinking as kids briefly entertain how they would write on a given topic. At first, writing circles need to be told in advance how they will share some writing from their circle with the whole class. "Okay, when we share today, let's hear a few golden sentences from each circle." Or, "Madame Chairperson, let's have a new nomination today. Someone from your circle who hasn't shared with the whole class recently." (Nominations

and golden sentences are explained in Chapter 9.) When kids have learned a repertoire of ways to share writing with the whole class, they are ready to decide as a group how they will give everyone a view into their writing circle.

- Don't lose the "think-back." It's sometimes a race against time at the end of writing circles—especially if kids have a lot to share. Don't let the reflection get lost in the shuffle.

Establishing Expectations

Teacher and student expectations about what happens in writing circles vary from situation to situation. The important thing is that these expectations be clearly set out, clarified, revised, and kept alive through group process. Here's how teacher Nona Schrader goes about it:

Before starting writing circles I established my expectations for their writing:

Legibility counts
Date each entry
Write out the topic
Write a minimum of one-half page.

On the first day of our writing circles we also formed groups and established group expectations. Students chose their own groups of four students. They are more likely to share their writing with a group of their choosing.

I then directed each group to write Group Expectations at the top of the next clean page and establish four group expectations. We used this process in literature circles, so they were familiar with it. I gave them the example of using good listening skills as a behavior.

Each group read aloud their expectations.

Each group then added one new expectation to their list after listening to the other groups.

Each group also chose a taskmaster to keep the group on track. I directed the taskmaster to develop a nonverbal signal to quiet down the group.

Each group also chose a reporter to share writing topics with the class.

Premeditating

When writing circles announce their next topic, make note of the topic of the circle you want to join for the next meeting. You might want to join a circle simply because their writing idea appeals to you. Or maybe it's time for a circle to move on from "Hannah Montana," and you want to be there when they decide their next topic. Joining different circles lets you know what's working and what could be better.

Solving Problems

After three or four writing circle meetings, hold a class discussion focused on time management. Ask kids to suggest solutions to problems and make the necessary adjustments together as a class.

Teaching

It is writing circles—not writing *in* circles! Take writing to the next level through your minilessons, one-on-one interactions, fishbowl conferences, and by actively participating in a series of writing circles. Be attuned to group dynamics and use group process to solve problems. If circles seem to be stuck in the same topics or genres, present a new-topic workshop to reinvigorate the selection process. If circles seem to be moving more toward voting than achieving consensus, stage a fishbowl conference on arriving at a consensus. Be alert for minilesson topics as you move from circle to circle. Have brief reinforcing conferences with kids and circles of kids.

Writing circles are a way to talk about all aspects of writing with kids in a comfortable, nonthreatening, engaged way. Point out examples of good writing. As you move from circle to circle, note what kids are learning about writing and small-group dynamics. Draw on these observations for minilessons and conferences. Numerous teachable moments regarding writing and small-group dynamics will present themselves. Keep your own writing circle notebook. While you're at it, grow a third ear out the back of your head and listen to how the other writing circles are going.

Assessing

Make clear to kids that they are responsible for keeping their own writing circle records. Help them become accurate historians of their writing circle experience. The place that holds this history is the writing circle notebook. Included in the notebook are drafts and think-back reflections for each writing circle meeting: circle name, topic, response, reflection, whether they were first writer or timekeeper, and whether they shared their writing with the whole class.

Participating in writing circles allows you to learn from and about the kids in that day's circle. In your writing circle notebook (see the anecdotal record discussion in Chapter 11), identify the kids you've observed and make some notes about them as writers and as members of the writing circle. These notes are valuable as you plan your conferences, assessments, and minilessons.

Thinking Back

Reflect on your own and kids' experience with writing circles. Share your observations with kids. Use reflections and observations to refine the writing circle process in your class. Jot down observational notes about the day's writing circle experience in general and what you noticed about the kids in the circle you joined in particular. (But don't turn low-risk writing high-risk by writing these observations while kids are sharing and responding to one another's writing.) Let's check in with Nona Schrader again:

> Last year I scheduled writing circles twice a week as students were becoming familiar with the process, so that it stays fresh in their minds. Two days in a row is best. We start by sharing the writing in the groups, discussing the writing as a class, and then choosing a new topic before the end of class, with time to write then and there. The next day we review the sharing process, listen, share our reflections, and again choose a new topic. Our class periods are forty-two minutes long, and we spend an entire period on writing circles both days.
>
> This year I plan to do the same thing, but I will first spend more time examining writing samples to demonstrate the sharing/response process. Last year the students did a good job of reaching consensus on topics and doing the writing, but they were not detailed or in depth in their responses to the writing. Because they are not used to this format, I need to model it more effectively using my own writing. I'll write about one of their topics, put my writing on the SMART Board, and then demonstrate a variety of ways someone might respond to my writing. I'll also have a preselected group take part in a fishbowl demonstration.

How About the Kids?

> Student: "We get to share our writing with other people and get a little time to relax and listen to other pieces."

To an outsider, it might look as if the kids are also just kicking back and enjoying writing and talking about their writing. Which is also true—and all too rare. But there's more to it than that. They're being good students.

Writing

Kids write a response for each idea their circle chooses. The writing kids share will generally be in draft form—with little revision or editing—similar in spirit to Donald Graves' "ten-minute writes" (but not limited to ten minutes). The idea is for kids to explore a point of view, opinion, experience with, and/or thoughts they have about the topic. "Draft" does not necessarily mean "short, brief, and undeveloped." In writing circles, kids try out different writing styles and points of view, explore their writing potential, set off on adventures of discovery. It's hard to explore in a sentence or two; a brief get-it-over-with response isn't much of an adventure. In writing circles, kids are expected to write, take writing risks, and see themselves as writers.

> Student: "Writing circles enabled me to write different types of writing and I actually took time to think over what I am writing about."

Creating New Writing Ideas

Kids are responsible for coming up with new writing ideas for their circle. When kids meet in their circles, they each have at least one new topic suggestion written down in their writing circle notebook. New writing ideas are prompted by other writing circle topics, topic-search workshops, and the growing list of Things I Want to Write About that kids keep in their writing circle notebook.

Making a Good Faith Effort

In order for kids to benefit from writing circles, they need to participate in the full writing circle process. This includes writing, sharing, and responding; putting forward new topics; working productively to reach consensus; participating in whole-class sharing, fishbowl conferences, and minilessons; keeping a writing circle notebook; and volunteering to take turns as first writer and timekeeper. Write, share, respond, and reflect. These are the keys to becoming a better writer.

Being Good Historians

Kids are responsible for keeping their own records—for documenting their good faith effort—in their writing circle notebook. Documentation includes the drafts and finished pieces they've written; the times they served as first writer or timekeeper or read their writing to the whole class; their new writing ideas; the types of responses they tried; and their regular think-back reflections.

Showing Respect

Respect includes listening to one another, focusing on positive response, and working to make every kid in the circle feel equal and included. Respecting kids in the circle means respecting the writing they produce as well. Each kid's writing deserves to be shared, listened to carefully, and given an encouraging response.

Building Community

4

In productive classrooms, teachers don't just teach children skills; they
build emotionally and relationally healthy learning communities.
　　—Peter H. Johnston

Is your classroom "too hot," "too cold," or "just right" for writing circles?
Writing circles flourish in classrooms where kids have fun working together, feel comfortable sharing their ideas and feelings, share a sense of
cooperation and community, and are comfortable quick-writing, drafting,
and exploring new topics. An added benefit of building community and
writing confidence are the numerous writing topics and ideas that emerge.

This chapter suggests strategies (often featuring writing) that give kids
good experiences working together and learning about one another. The
idea isn't to use each of the strategies. Most teachers have their own tried-
and-true community-building activities. The point is to increase kids' comfort with drafting and generating topic ideas in preparation for writing circles. Some strategies might seem more applicable for specific grade levels,
but they all easily adapt to any level.

Drawing the Circle: Community-Building Strategies

There are a number of strategies you can use to welcome every student as
a valued member of your learning community. The idea is not to start building community immediately before beginning writing circles. What works
best is to incorporate the strategies all year long so that when kids do start
writing circles the classroom climate is "just right."

Interviews

If kids aren't comfortable having conversations with one another—speaking and listening—it's going to be difficult for them to learn from one
another. When kids interview one another, they enter into an informal

social compact that implicitly holds that all students have interesting things to say as long as they are taken seriously (listened to). When kids regularly interview one another, they become much better at responding to one another and to one another's writing. The keys to interviewing are to ask good questions, be nonjudgmental, and to listen—good hallmarks of writing circles as well.

Kids enjoy learning more about one another, connecting. Tap into the feeling of individuality within a community by having pairs of kids interview each other and then introduce their partner to the entire class. Interview questions can be generated by the class. What do kids want to know about their classmates? Generating these questions is an opportune moment to begin defining what constitutes a good (instead of a dead-end) question.

Seize opportunities for kids to interview one another regularly about their personal experiences and history, their thoughts about learning, reading, writing, life. Instead of asking the questions yourself, have kids ask one another, jot down responses, and ask more questions in return—not questions that are accusations, but questions seeking to learn more, better understand, and wonder about—searching for clarification and connection. For younger kids, use turn-and-talks as a way to get comfortable with different classmates before taking on more organized interviews.

Proust Questionnaire

The Proust questionnaire is an interview subgenre with its own Wikipedia entry. In the late nineteenth century it was fashionable to play a parlor game in which answers to a specific list of questions were thought to reveal character and personality. French writer Marcel Proust (*Remembrance of Things Past*) answered such a questionnaire when he was thirteen and again when he was twenty. Over time, the two questionnaires combined and evolved into what is known as the Proust questionnaire. The Proust questionnaire is a regular feature in several magazines (*Vanity Fair*, most notably) and the culminating part of the interview format James Lipton uses on the TV program *Inside the Actors Studio*.

The conventional Proust questionnaire (like the one in *Vanity Fair*) has twenty-five questions. The adaptation used by James Lipton has ten. The twenty questions presented in Figure 4-1 (albeit too many for any single interview or class discussion) merge the two in language accessible to all

Proust Questionnaire Adapted for the Classroom

1. What is your favorite word?

2. What sound do you love?

3. What sound do you hate?

4. What is your most treasured possession?

5. Where would you like to live?

6. What are your favorite books?

7. What do you most dislike?

8. What's your dream of happiness?

9. What's your greatest fear?

10. Who or what do you love?

11. When you grow up, what do you want to be?

12. If you could be an animal, what animal would you be?

13. What's your favorite music?

14. What's your favorite color?

15. What's your favorite flower?

16. How do you feel today?

17. What's your favorite food and drink?

18. What's your idea of a fun time?

19. If you could change one thing about yourself, what would it be?

20. What phrase, nickname, motto, or saying describes you?

students. They are the kinds of questions kids often arrive at on their own as potential writing circle topics. Narrow the questions to five or six you think will be most productive, or better yet, have kids select five or six questions from the larger list to answer. They can then choose one of their answers as the topic for a five-minute quick-write to share with their interview partner(s) or small group.

Let kids know that answering the questionnaire connects them to one of the world's greatest writers, a large Internet community, the popular press, and a high-brow weekly television program. Encourage kids to note questions they might want to write about later in their writing circles.

When Proust answered the questionnaire, he revised or ignored some of the questions and wrote a few of his own ("What is your favorite bird?"). What new question would kids in your class ask? Encourage kids to save their answers in their writing circle notebook. They contain numerous writing topics and are a way to measure changing values and self-perception over time. And who knows? Proust's copy of the answers he wrote to similar questions when he was twenty sold at auction in 2003 for a quarter of a million dollars.

Three Facts and a Fiction

This variation on an oft-used ice breaker (kids love to call it Three Truths and One Lie) builds community and deepens kids' understanding of the how of writing. (The truth/falsehood, fact/fiction confluence has given rise to its own genre: *faction*.)

In groups of four or five, kids jot down three facts about themselves or their life and one fiction—in random order. Kids then take turns sharing their entire list with their group. Group members can ask questions about what's on the list, but the writer does not respond other than to note the questions. After all the kids have shared their list and listened to questions, each chooses one (fact or fiction) from their own list to write about. Give kids enough time (fifteen minutes or so) to get involved in their story. Kids then read their fact or fiction draft to their group and the group votes "fact" or "fiction." Some true stories end up being judged "didn't happen," and some pure fiction is rated "the truest thing I ever heard." This is one of the things writing's all about: creating credibility.

Let's play Truth or Fiction with these three pieces from a tenth-grade language arts class:

Take Your Mark

The moment right before our race is the most nerve-racking part, and walking up to your lane and not knowing if you will win or lose tears me apart. My heart beats faster and faster, and I just can't wait to get the race over with. All I can think about is getting first place and beating my best time. Once the official blows the whistle and signals for us to step up onto the slippery blocks, my adrenaline hits the roof, but I've learned to love it. "Take your mark!" says the official. The only way to describe that feeling is as if you are at the tippy-top of the highest rollercoaster ever made, waiting for the very second you start to race back to solid ground. At that very moment everything goes silent, I can feel the people cheering but all I hear is my racing heart and heavy breathing. My life seems to be stuck in slow motion. Once the official hits the buzzer, my body automatically pushes itself off of the block, almost as if it's programmed to do so. The only thing I have left to do is prove how hard I have worked in practice and take that first place title.

I use every ounce of energy in me to swim as fast as I can. I think about nothing else but finishing. I get to the wall and do my flip turn, and push off with all my might. While underwater, I try to hold my breath for as long as I can, but the first breath I take is such a relief. I'm on my final lap, and I take a glance at the wall only a few feet in front of me. The timers get ready to slam down on their stopwatches. I take my last bit of energy out on the wall; my hand goes numb from hitting it so hard. Looking over to my right or left, I see no one, and it is the best feeling in the world to know that I reached my goal.

If I Was Spiderman

I climb high above the city using my worn hands, which somehow are able to hold on to the tired bricks of this old building. As I reach the top, I see Chicago at its finest. I wonder why anyone would want to live anywhere but here. Lights flash everywhere, cars honk every once and a while, and the bright crescent moon hovers just above Lake Michigan. My eyes are growing hard to keep open. I fling myself over to Navy Pier and make myself a comfortable web to sleep on as I listen to the waves crashing against the sand and think how great my life is.

I wake up in a panic. Sirens are blaring in my ears. Police cars surround the old bank down the street. Without thinking twice, I swoop in through the window and the glass shatters to the marble floors. All eyes are on me now. The robbers are looking at me, their faces hidden behind masks that looked like they were painted by kindergartners. They look at me, fooling themselves by actually thinking they can take me on, but I know I can beat them. The first to come at me is a short fat guy who takes off his mask to reveal his face. A thick mustache lays just above his upper lip and his sausage fingers flick the still burning cigarette to the ground. He ordered himself a quick wake-up call and found himself flying out the window. The next few came all at once but I managed them all. One found his head through the wall and one dangled from the crystal chandelier hanging by a golden chain from the ceiling. And all the others, let's just say they had to make a pit stop at the hospital before making it to their new home (also known as jail). Sometimes I feel bad for hurting people like this, but once I think of all the horrible things they do, I feel better about it. The few hostages shook my hand and thanked me for saving their lives. I'm used to all the thank-yous by now.

This whole bank thing took longer than expected so I headed back to my house to freshen up before I went out with a couple girls. My superhero charm always gets them. Today's work was easy. But as for tomorrow, I can never predict what I'm in for.

Truth or Fib

My most terrifying day happened on a cold winter morning in fourth grade. I was peacefully walking down the sidewalk, heading toward school. The day was dark, the sky full of dull gray clouds with no sign of a morning sunrise.

A soft rattling noise caught my attention. It sounded like a jingle of keys, only softer and distant. Curious, I turned casually over my shoulder, unaware of the short, ugly monster I would face. There, a block away, stood the chubby pit bull. He was the color of sand, and had a white patch over one eye. The distant jingle I had heard was his steel silver collar rattling as he stepped closer toward the edge of the street. I did a quick glance around the street, but saw no sign of an owner. It was just me and the pit bull, all alone.

He challenged me with his beady eyes. His mouth hung open, so that his tongue dangled over the corner of his mouth. A cloud of heavy steam came from his hot breath as he edged closer toward me.

I did a silent prayer, hoping the dog would turn the corner. My hopefulness crashed as the dog's short, stocky legs began jogging straight toward me.

My heart was pounding as if I ran a mile, and my stomach growled with uneasiness. I could see the hatred in his eyes, and knew he wanted more than a friendly pat on the head. Before I knew what I was doing, my feet slipped against the pavement as I ran. If I wasn't carrying my heavy book bag, I probably could have run faster.

But I was too tired and began to slow down. Heart pounding, I gazed over my shoulder. How could a dog possibly run so fast?

He was already a few feet away. He grabbed the edge of my jeans with his teeth, and tugged me to the ground. For such a small animal, he had amazing strength. As much as I tried kicking free, he had a firm grip on my shoe and had no intentions of letting go.

Then my hopes flared as I heard the wonderful sound of a car engine. The driver was a middle-aged woman, who parked on the edge of the curb and came to my aid. She also carried a tall black umbrella, and began hitting the dog furiously with it. Whimpering, the dog finally let go of my foot.

We watched with amazement as the dog ran between us and across the street. I never walked to school again.

Credibility and belief depend on how the writer uses language, on how words combine with one another. There are qualities of good writing that transcend genre, situation, and, in this case, reality itself: details, something important to say, and voice. What makes a piece of writing "believable"? Building community through writing allows us to provide a positive successful writing experience, strengthen the social connections among kids, and talk about writing—and what constitutes good writing—in a fun, adventurous atmosphere. It foreshadows the writing circles that are to come.

Co-Writing

Writing in the real world is increasingly co-authored. Co-writing is fun, motivates kids, creates synergy, and combats procrastination. Co-writing is an opportunity for kids to work together rather than compete. The following are two favorites.

Chain Story

In this collaborative writing activity, groups of four or five kids sit in a circle and each writes the start of a story. After a specific time, the papers are passed to the adjacent student. The next student reads the opening and extends the story and passes the paper again. The pattern repeats until all the stories have gone full circle and each student has their original paper. The result is a collection of stories, each unique, written by the same group of kids. Kids remain in the circle, reading and talking about the stories. Each circle can then choose one of their chain stories to revise and refine as a group—making the writing more fluid, taking out contradictions and things that just don't seem to work, clarifying details, and giving their story a title. This process works best when you can make copies for each kid— or the writing is done online.

Chain stories depend on kids' understanding and following specific directions. You might start out with the opening lines of an unfamiliar children's story, a compelling photo, a mysterious statement ("Nothing was ever the same after . . ."), or a student-generated sentence. Give kids a specific time to write their link before passing the paper on to the next kid. Have the kids sit in a circle because it makes passing the paper easy. "Okay, everyone pass to the right." Remember to increase the amount of time as the stories develop—kids need time to read what has already been written as well as draft their contribution. If kids have one minute to write their first contribution, they will probably need two or three minutes to read through and then write their final contribution. It's essential that kids pass their paper in a timely manner or the stories will back up, causing anxiety rather than delight. Tell kids they need to pass their papers when time is called, whether they are finished or not. If they end in midsentence, the next contributor picks the writing up there, completes the sentence, and continues writing until the next rotation. As kids write, keep track of the time and head off potential backups. Younger kids might each write a single sentence every time the papers are passed along. For older kids, provide longer time allotments for more development (perhaps a paragraph instead of a single sentence). Given their multiple authorship, chain stories often develop in unpredictable and surprising ways. To keep stories from degenerating (more of a risk with older students), be clear about content and language from the outset: "The story can be funny, scary, sad, happy, mysterious. . . . You are the authors! (*Please—nothing obscene or offensive.*)"

Incomplete Manuscripts

Our innate curiosity and desire to resolve a feeling of suspense make us want to finish a story. Take advantage of that motivation with opportunities for kids to co-write the next scene or the end of a good read-aloud or the story behind a compelling illustration. A classic invitation to write the missing story is *The Mysteries of Harris Burdick*, by Chris Van Allsburg. As Van Allsburg (1984) maintains in his introduction, the book's fourteen drawings (with titles and captions) were left with a children's book publisher by their creator, Harris Burdick. Burdick promised to return with the accompanying stories the next morning, but "was never heard from again. . . . To this day Harris Burdick remains a complete mystery." Indeed, as Van Allsburg states, it is "difficult . . . to look at the drawings and their captions without imagining a story." Have kids choose one of the drawings and do just that. Unless you want fourteen groups, narrow the drawing choices so there'll be three to five kids in each group. Kids choose their group by choosing the drawing they want to work with. Encourage kids to discuss what they see in the drawing, what the drawing makes them think about, and what the caption means before they start their story. Kids write their story by themselves or collaboratively.

Treasure Hunt

Have kids write *one* interesting fact about themselves on an index card: something they did, something they think about, something that no one would guess about them, something as simple as how many brothers or sisters they have or the name of their pet cat, Puff Daddy. Collect the cards and make a handout listing the facts alongside space for kids to match the fact with a student's name (see the example in Figure 4-2).

Figure 4-2. Sample Treasure Hunt Handout

Name(s)	Fact
_____	I was born in Texas.
_____	My favorite place is Disneyworld.
_____	I have two brothers and a sister.
_____	Strawberry ice cream's the best.

continues

_____   I tweet.

_____   My cat's named Puff Daddy.

_____   I am learning to play guitar.

_____   I hate lima beans.

_____   I am a Packer fan.

Kids ricochet around the room finding out who matches the fact and writing in the names. Set a time limit (ten minutes or so). Often a fact can be matched with more than one student. Even though Tammy thinks "Strawberry ice cream's the best," her favorite place might also be Disneyworld. There's probably no one else in the class with a cat named Puff Daddy, however. There's a story behind each fact, a number of candidates for the writing circle topic lists, and newfound and often unexpected connections among kids.

My Name

Like the rest of the chapters in *The House on Mango Street*, by Sandra Cisneros (1984), "My Name" is brief and memorable. The narrator's name is Esperanza. "In English my name means hope. In Spanish it means too many letters" (10). Esperanza explores her name from a number of angles, including literal meaning and all sorts of associations. The name's a "muddy color"; it's "like the number 9"; it sounds "like sobbing." She traces the name's family history ("It was my great-grandmother's name"), which leads to minihistories of her grandmother and grandfather. She confronts her feelings about the name and what it has come to mean for her: "I have inherited her name, but I don't want to inherit her place by the window" (11). The chapter ends with Esperanza's desire to "baptize myself under a new name, a name more like the real me, the one nobody sees" (11). For this new name she chooses "Zeze the X."

Names are, of course, important to kids: names they have, names they want, nicknames, middle names, the variant spellings of their name. What name do they want to be called in class? In writing circles, kids are going to be working together—talking to one another, reading and responding to one another's writing—so it's important that everyone knows one another's names. The name that feels comfortable in the classroom.

Have the class stand in a circle. Go around the circle, each person saying something about their name. Where did it come from? Are they named after anyone? What's their middle name? How about nicknames? Do they like their name? What kind of associations do they have with their name? What name do they want to be called in class? This is time consuming and slow going if each kid addresses all of these aspects. Limit kids to one statement about their name to keep the sharing brief and manageable.

Kids can also research their name. They can interview their parents, family members, or guardians regarding the history of their name and perhaps find out something unusual: "It was my mother's favorite soap opera character." They can research famous namesakes and investigate some unknown family history. Send kids to Web sites like http://babynamesworld.parentsconnect.com to find out more. Remember there are a number of names here to work with—first name, middle name, last name, nickname—you name it.

Pen Name

There's benefit in getting kids to see themselves as authors and understand that writers incorporate different voices and styles in their writing. The separation of the writer from the writing is a complex issue, and one that's highly entertaining to think about.

Take the case of Theodor Seuss Geisel, once a student at Dartmouth College and editor-in-chief of the college humor magazine, *The Dartmouth Jack-O-Lantern*. When Geisel was caught hosting a drinking party during Prohibition, he was ordered to resign from the magazine. Geisel did not want to resign, so he continued to write and work on the magazine under the pen name Dr. Seuss.

There are many reasons why authors choose to write under a pen name. Maybe they think their real name won't sell books the way a name like Mark Twain did (and does). Maybe they don't want to be confused with an already famous author. It would be difficult to send out a manuscript written by another Ernest Hemingway. Historically, female writers used male pen names to counteract sexism (Mary Ann Evans wrote as George Eliot in the nineteenth century). Writers have adopted pen names to reflect their dominant writing genre (Pearl Grey became western novelist Zane Grey), or to make a memorable impression (Avi is the pen name of Edward Irving Wortis; Lemony Snicket, that of Daniel Handler).

What pen name would kids choose for themselves? Encourage them to think of a name that is unique and appropriate for the writer they want to be. Have kids, in small groups, share their pen names and reflect on what they think it would take to become "the writer they want to be." This is an opportunity to talk with kids about writing as a process for developing an identity, as well as some practical things writers do to become stronger writers.

Headline News

On a Friday, bring in a daily newspaper and share some of the headlines with kids and discuss what constitutes a good headline (simple, direct, a strong active verb). The idea is that kids then come to school on Monday with "headline news" about something that happened to them over the weekend, for example:

Runaway Dog Found at Neighbors
Wallet Lost at Movies: Investigation Underway
Unknown Sub Scores Winning Basket

On Monday morning, each kid reads their headline while their classmates guess at the rest of the story. The headline maker finally sets the record straight with their real weekend news—either in a verbal exercise or through writing.

Listen to the Rainstorm

Everyone loves a good rainstorm—as long as there's no flooding. Get kids up from their desks facing each other in a circle (what else?). This particular "rainstorm" consists of five sounds:

1. Palms of one's hands rubbing together.
2. Fingers snapping.
3. Hands clapping (slowly, not in unison).
4. Palms of one's hands slapping one's thighs—in somewhat faster alternating rhythm.
5. Feet stomping.

Start by practicing the individual sounds. The idea is for someone to initiate the first sound (palms rubbing together) and the kid to the right to pick up the sound, then the kid to that person's right, and so on. As the sound travels around the circle, it becomes louder as each kid joins in.

When the sound comes back around to the kid who initiated it, she or he initiates the second sound (fingers snapping), which then starts to build as it moves around the circle. The process continues with each sound to the inevitable thunderous downpour of everyone's stomping feet. When the stomping sound comes full circle back to the first person, he or she stops stomping and stands silent, then the person to the right falls silent, and so on around the circle as the sound of the thunderstorm gradually fades into the distance.

After they've "dried off," ask kids how the rainstorm activity made them feel, and/or what it made them think about. Some kids will undoubtedly talk about times they got soaked, and many will say it was fun and want to do it again. The Listen to the Rainstorm activity teaches kids about the power of working together. One person snapping her fingers cannot cause a rainstorm. One raindrop does not a thunderstorm make. It takes everyone working together to create something as beautiful as this sudden change in classroom weather.

You can sound this note again when you introduce kids to writing circles. Make it thunder once more in your class. After the storm has passed, talk to kids again about the mysteries and power of group dynamics. To emphasize the "listening" aspect of the rainstorm activity, have kids try it with their eyes closed.

Diversity Circle

Prior to this activity, ask kids to freewrite for a few minutes on the topic "what you can't tell about me from looking at me." The prewriting helps generate ideas about what to share.

Then place chairs in a circle—one fewer chair than the number of students. The person not sitting stands in the center of the circle and states something about himself or herself, an "I" statement ("I have two brothers," "I've been on a train"). It should be something specific that might be shared by some of the other kids in the class but not so specific as to exclude everyone. The statement "I have a dog" will probably be true for a number of kids in the circle; "I have a dog named Thunder" will isolate rather than connect.

If this statement is also true for other kids sitting in the circle, those kids have to jump up from their seat and move to another chair. The only empty chairs will be those vacated by someone else for whom the statement is true. Kids have to move quickly, since the kid in the center of the circle will also be trying to sit down. After the dust has settled, the person left standing starts the next round. If no one stands up after the person in the middle makes their personal statement, applaud him for his true uniqueness and ask him to share a second different personal statement.

You might lay some ground rules about walking instead of running, no shoving or tripping. After about ten minutes, talk about the activity as a class. What did they like and dislike about the experience? What kinds of things did they notice? When did more kids move? When did fewer? How did it feel to be alone in the center of the circle? How much do they know about one another? How valid are the assumptions they make about one another? On what do they base these assumptions? What kinds of groups are they part of? How does being part of a group shape attitudes? Is group membership self-selected? Can it be assigned?

Diversity circles are a harbinger of writing circles: what would happen if we grouped ourselves according to what we wanted to write about?

Six-Word Memoir

As the story goes, Ernest Hemingway was once challenged to write a novel in six words. His response: "For sale: baby shoes, never worn." A recent book, *Not Quite What I Was Planning: Six-Word Memoirs by Writers Famous and Obscure* (*Smith Magazine*, 2008), contains almost a thousand of these little gems. The six-word memoir has attracted teachers as well. "The Short, Happy Lives of Teachers" is the six-word title of a collection of six-word stories "of your own teaching life" published by *Teacher Magazine*. Dayle: "Making a difference, leaving a legacy." Donna: "First-class life with second graders!" Karen in Indiana: "Portal to the world beyond cornfields."

Everyone has a story to tell. Have kids list some favorite stories about their own life, select one, and capture its essence in six words. The resulting "micromemoirs" offer insight into each kid's life, as well as teach lessons about word choice, clarity, and story dynamics (conflict, suspense, resolution). This is also a rare opportunity for every kid to feel successful as an editor, looking hard at every single word.

The six-word memoir is an ideal writing circle community-building activity because (1) it helps kids feel comfortable and engaged with one another; (2) it gives each kid a successful authentic writing experience; and (3) it motivates future writing. Here are some examples created by sixth graders:

I thought I could. I did.
Moving from place to place. Alone.
Feeling it's my birthday every day.
Trying harder. Studying longer. Making grade.
No way out. No way in.
Shy me waiting for new friends.

Six-word memoirs call out for elaboration and can serve as a default writing idea if a writing circle can't settle on a new topic. It's fascinating to have kids write about someone else's six-word memoir as well. The six words suggest a certain narrative framework that somehow creates more room for the imagination. Illustrated six-word memoirs displayed as a gallery walk (see Chapter 9) can also provide visual inspiration for future writing.

"Did being in a writing circle make you a better writer?"

"Yes, because writing circles let me express myself and open up. After hearing others' stories, you open up to more words, styles, and topics."

Together we write.

5

Writeable Moments

Writing created in a writing circle is usually a draft, often (but not always) written quickly. Even though the writing may be produced quickly, kids generally think a lot about how they are going to write about the chosen topic. The result is writing that's often creative, with a strong voice.

Low-Risk Writing Activities

Writing circles depend on kids' feeling comfortable, not frozen by fear that they will make a mistake. If your kids have already participated in writing workshop or you've engaged in some of the activities featured in Chapter 4, they are most likely already on friendly terms with writing and the writing process. The following writing activities reduce writing anxiety and help kids become more at ease writing a draft. They also provide ways for kids to discover new writing ideas to explore. Remember, low-risk writing is not necessarily low-quality. It simply means the pressure is off; each kid can be successful and take writing risks without fear of penalty or failure.

Freewrites

Call them brief writes, quick-writes, messy writes, freefall writing, or five-minute writes, freewrites are quick and uncensored—writing with the superego turned off. Frequent freewriting is one of the best ways to get students comfortable with the exploratory rough drafts they bring to writing circles. Frequent freewriting is also one of the best ways for kids to find out what they are thinking. As Peter Elbow states in *Writing with Power* (1981), "Freewriting is the easiest way to get words on paper and the best all-around practice in writing that I know. . . . Freewriting exercises are pushups in withholding judgment as you produce so that afterward you can judge better" (13–14). These brief, timed writings show kids how it feels to "just write," and the resulting fluidity carries over to the writing they do in writing circles.

The only way to fail at freewriting is not to do it. Start with three to five minutes and increase over time. Encourage kids to let the writing take its own direction. Once they start their freewrite, kids need to keep writing without making corrections or taking time out to second-guess themselves. No stopping to "fix things" like spelling, punctuation, paragraphing, and grammar. If kids get stuck, they continue to write—the last word over again until something else comes to mind, about what frustration and futility feel like, or "I'm sure I'll think of something." And they will. Freewriting is private and not shared unless the writer volunteers. Not collected. Not graded. The entire class, including the teacher, enjoys five minutes or so of unrepentant, anxiety-reduced writing. A written sigh of relief.

Directed Freewrites

When freewriting is generated by something specific (often something connected to content), it generally becomes more directed—focused but not narrow. Directed freewrites encourage kids to continue writing with energy and freedom. In a directed freewrite, kids might all start off in the same general writing territory, but each quickly blazes an individual path. When fifth graders are asked to jot down what they are thinking about at the end of a chapter in *Maniac McGee*, for instance, the drafts quickly become individual in idea, language, and development.

Empower the class by having groups of kids decide on the day's directed freewriting topic by consensus. The resulting directed freewriting can also serve as a basis for a discussion about what makes a good writing topic. If you want kids to share part or all of their directed freewriting, tell them that before they start writing.

Written Conversations

It's not true that "kids today" don't like to write. They might not like to write a certain way, but just watch them email, blog, text, or twitter. Tap into that kind of enthusiasm to communicate by giving kids opportunities to write back and forth about compelling issues. In the question/answer classroom of the distant past (hope!), the teacher asks the important question and a handful of kids compete with raised hands to answer—or more correctly, to guess at the teacher's answer. Kids who don't raise their hand aren't going to play and pretty much lose interest. When one eager student is called on and delivers a really good answer—the "correct" answer—

the waving hands of the other adventurous kids—first tentatively, then quickly—are reeled in, a visual withering of inquiry. When you want to ask all the kids in the class a provocative, interesting question that should promote discussion, by all means ask the question—but have *all* the kids write their answer, hand their response to a partner, read through what their partner has written, and write back (all in about the same amount of time it takes to pull out the "right" answer in a whole-class "discussion"). This is not just one piece of paper per group; each kid starts their own sheet and is always reading or writing.

In written dialogue like this, *all* kids get to write their answer. Written dialogues make for better writers, better communicators, better community members, and better learners. Written dialogues are also a good way for kids to start to relate with one another *through* their writing.

Once kids are comfortable with written dialogues, expand the experience through group write-arounds, in which each kid in the groups initiates a piece of writing that is then passed successively to everyone else in the group, each kid adding their point of view to the evolving text. If there are five kids in the group, there will be five evolving texts. Write-arounds are similar in structure to chain stories (Chapter 4) except that write-arounds generally produce conversations around a topic rather than an evolving narrative. In a write-around, kids respond to one another's questions, observations, and points of view. The dynamics of a write-around are like those of a writing circle—drafting, sharing drafts, responding, and working together—and are a useful touchstone once writing circles are humming along.

Stack the Deck for Writing Circles

When kids form writing circles, it's important for them to have a list of writing ideas to draw on. Some of these ideas will come from previous writing workshops, their writer's notebooks, class discussions, and read-alouds. A things-to-write-about list—whether kept mentally or on paper—is part of every writer's life and central to being in a writing circle. An essential part of the writing circle dynamic involves kids' seeing the writing potential in one another's topics. "Let children help each other," Donald Graves advises. "Children pick up a heavy percentage of topic ideas from each other" (1983, 28).

Demonstrate the potential of kids working *together* to discover things to write about by stacking the topic deck:

1. Give kids four index cards and have them write a good writing topic on each card. (Note: A "good writing topic" is something kids want to write about.)
2. Collect the cards and arrange kids in groups of four.
3. Deal three cards to each student and stack the four extra cards face down in the middle of each group.
4. Kids look at the three cards they've been dealt, keep one of the cards, and pass the remaining two cards to the person on their right.
5. Kids look at the two new cards they've been passed, keep one, and pass the card they don't want to the person on their right.
6. Kids can either keep this final card or discard it and pick one off the top of the four-card stack in the center of the table.
7. Each kid now has varying degrees of ownership over at least three writing topics. Kids choose one and tell the rest of their group why they chose that topic.
8. After all the group members have shared their topic and talked a little about why they chose it, they write about the topic for ten or fifteen minutes.
9. When kids have finished their writing, have a class discussion about the many opportunities for good writing that can be found in what initially might be viewed as unpromising topics.
10. Collect and keep the deck of topic cards as a resource; alternatively, provide a copy of all the writing topics suggested by the class for kids to keep in their writing circle notebook for later reference. When kids draw a blank for a new writing topic, they can fan through the topic deck (or skim the list in their notebook) and get new ideas.

You can reduce or increase the number of blank topic cards each kid receives, both initially and in their individual groups, depending on the grade level and situation.

List Poems

Shel Silverstein is a master of the list poem—a deceptively simple catalogue of details that magnifies meaning through its minimalist structure. Reading some of Silverstein's list poems to kids (favorites include "Listen to the Mustn'ts," "Mr. Grumpledump's Song," and "Sick") helps get them excited about writing a list poem of their own. Writing a list poem demonstrates the abundance of interesting things to write about and how close observation often produces surprising, compelling writing topics.

Almost any person, place, or thing, looked at closely enough, will yield interesting details that become even more interesting when isolated and arranged in a list poem. When you think about it, our lives are often organized and controlled by lists. Lists are everywhere. One can even write a list poem about lists:

A List of Lists

"To do"
Grocery
Wish
Food I Won't Eat
Things to Write About
What to Pack
Thank-You
Christmas
Places to See Before I Die
Bucket
Favorite Songs
Most Useless Items of Crapola
Ten Best Movies
What to Ask the Doctor
A List of Lists

Start kids off by having them jot down some places whose contents would be fun to inventory: purse, backpack, top drawer, locker, closet, storage unit, bookshelf, under the bed, in the medicine cabinet, a corner of the classroom, a garden. Try it yourself. Go to a small confined space of some kind and take a good hard look. For example:

Glove Compartment

They travel along with me every day:
registration and insurance card
small scissors
nut—no bolt
map that would've been handy last week if I'd remembered it was there

ice scraper
pocket owner's manual
Conway Twitty's Greatest Hits Vol. 3
empty Altoids tin box (made in Great Britain)
flashlight—needs battery
Villa Nova Pizza phone number
three pens
cracked pair of sunglasses
five fuses
eight pennies, a dime, and a quarter
key to something
no gloves

A list poem should be structured as an actual list. Stylistic consistencies—including repetition and parallel structure—contribute to the effect. No need to rhyme, and no required rhythm, although the iteration of a series of items often has an inherent rhythm. Each item on the list should be chosen for a specific reason—selected and positioned rather than swept up and dumped randomly on the page. It becomes easier to select and position the items in a list poem once the purpose of the list begins to reveal itself. As children's author Bruce Lansky notes (www.gigglepoetry.com), list poems are written to "tell you something, to point something out—'Look at this,' or 'Think about this.'" Often the last item of the list is significant, ironic, or funny.

Because we wanted students to be equipped when they met in writing circles for the first time, we spent time having students develop, in their writer's notebooks, possible lists of topics such as My Favorites, I'm an Expert, I'm Curious About, and Ten Things I Remember.
—Deborah Zaffiro

Writing the Walkshed

walkshed *n.*
"The area that can be conveniently reached on foot from a given geographic point. Compare with foodshed, the area sufficient to provide food for a given location, and viewshed, the landscape or topography visible from a given geographic point, especially one having aesthetic value. All are patterned after watershed." (Barrett 2007)

This is a good after-school assignment that combines close observation with some physical action. In this activity, kids go for a short walk. As they walk they list things, people, or events they find interesting. Afterward, kids share their lists in small groups and answer one another's informational questions. After a group discussion, kids choose one thing from their list and write about it for ten or fifteen minutes. They then return to their group and read their draft aloud.

Whole-class discussion can focus on the plenitude of writing topics that surround us, that inhabit us. Any number of kids can travel the same "walk-shed" and come up with very different lists and topics. As an overture to writing circles, encourage kids to compare the variety of their writing and how style, point of view, and form (genre) are individual to the writer.

Examining Attitudes Toward Writing

Writing circles are all about becoming better writers—which for many kids involves unpacking their attitudes toward writing. Have kids write on a piece of paper folded in half lengthwise: "What makes writing easy for me?" at the top of the first side of a sheet of paper and "What makes writing hard for me?" at the top of the other side. Then have them jot down things in the respective columns. Ask them to share their responses in groups, note common entries, and agree on three conditions in each category that are true for every member of the group. Then have all the groups display their lists and highlight those that are duplicated by another group. Point out how many of the "easy" conditions are incorporated into the structure of writing circles, thus giving kids a preview of the exciting writing adventures to come.

Personal Metaphor

This activity is an opportunity to teach some parts of speech (nouns, adjectives) and figures of speech (simile, metaphor), validate the importance of the visual image, and help kids learn more about one another.

1. Start by having kids list some adjectives and nouns that relate to them. Generally speaking, nouns define *who they are*, adjectives *how they see themselves*. Some nouns (and noun phrases) might be *student, basketball player, toy collector, video game player, fan of Harry Potter books, singer, dancer, daughter, son, brother, sister, dreamer.*

Some adjectives might be *happy, energetic, creative, thoughtful, hard-working, confident, lonely, friendly, carefree, positive, optimistic.*

2. Ask kids to look over their list and circle three words that best describe them.

3. With these words as a foundation, have kids compare themselves to a person, place, thing, or event using *like:* I am like a garden in bloom. I am like a high-flying kite. I am like a new pair of shoes. I am like a bridge over a river.

4. Have kids change this simile into a metaphor by taking out *like:* I am a garden in bloom. I am a high-flying kite. I am a new pair of shoes. I am a bridge over a river.

5. Finally, have kids draw a visual representation of this personal metaphor and use some of the words on their original list to expand the metaphor.

Examples are shown in Figures 5-1 and 5-2.

I am a Cactus

My small, pin like prickles often fend off attackers
that attempt to penetrate me. Nobody who endangers
me gets away without learning a small, maybe not
physical, lesson.

I have a rough outside skin, but I have room for a
small soft spot near my center.

Figure 5-1. Illustration and Text for "I am a Cactus"

Katie

I am a Never-Ending CD

My music brings comfort to those who hear it.

I am put in to a case describing who and what I play.

I can bring people together with the just the right song and the right time.

My music never stops.

I am a Never-Ending CD.

Figure 5-2. Illustration and Text for "I Am a Never-Ending CD"

"I Am From . . ."

The initial response to the question "Where are you from?" is usually a geographic location—a state, a city, a section of a city, a street, an address. On a deeper level, however, we are also created from our families, significant people in our lives, essential character-forming experiences, special events, and places.

Have kids make notes on various possibilities that help define where they're from. (They can generate some categories and ideas using the template in Figure 5-3.) Tell students that when they write their "I am from . . ." piece, they should repeat "I am from" to introduce each new idea. The repetition gives the writing a strong forward rhythm that provides continuity. Figure 5-4 is an "I am from . . ." piece written by a sixth grader.

"I Am From . . ." Template

When a new friend asks "Where are you from?" what do I say?

I am from . . . [a favorite family tradition]

I am from . . . [special people in my family—past and present]

I am from . . . [a favorite place as experienced through the senses]

sight   smell   taste   hearing   touch

I am from . . . [a favorite family story]

I am from . . . [something my family holds dear]

Figure 5-3   *Writing Circles* by Jim Vopat (Heinemann: Portsmouth, NH); © 2009

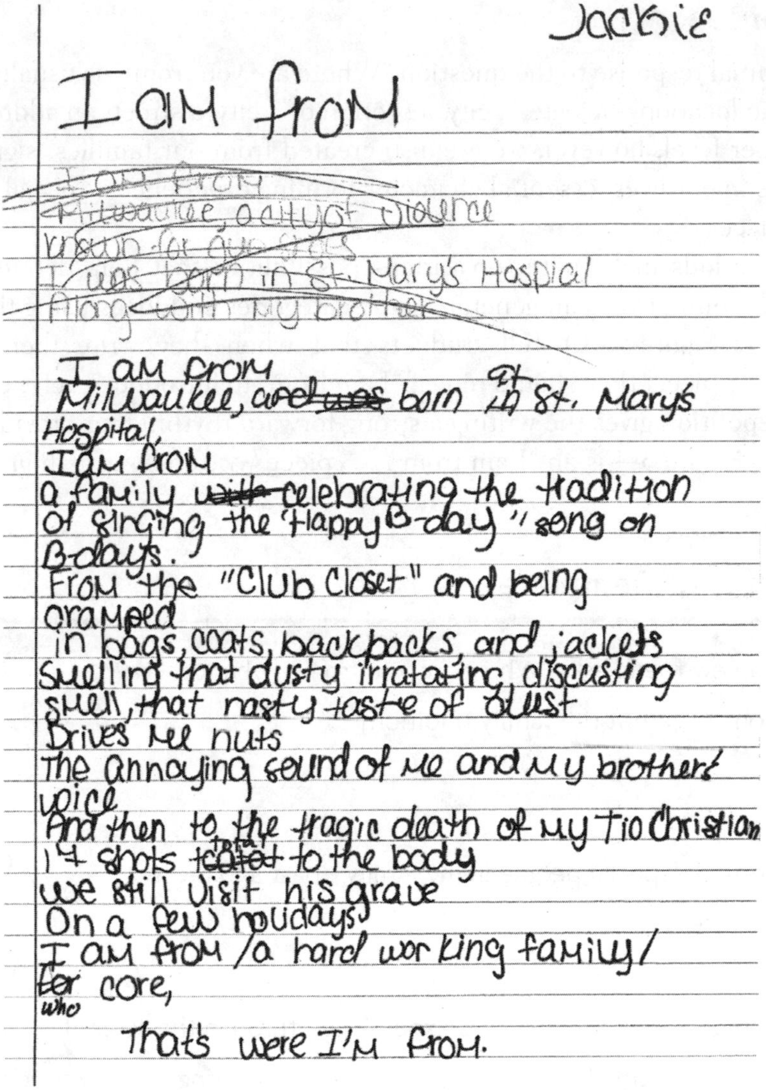

Jackie

I am from

~~I am from~~
~~Milwaukee, a city of violence~~
~~known for gangs~~
~~I was born in St. Mary's Hospial~~
~~along with my brother~~

I am from
Milwaukee, ~~and was~~ born at in St. Mary's
Hospital,
I am from
a family ~~with~~ celebrating the tradition
of singing the "Happy B-day" song on
B-days.
From the "Club Closet" and being
cramped
in bags, coats, backpacks, and jackets
smelling that dusty irratating discusting
smell, that nasty taste of dust
Drives me nuts
The annoying sound of me and my brothers
voice
And then to the tragic death of my Tio Christian
14 shots to the body
We still visit his grave
On a few holidays.
I am from /a hard working family/
to core,
who
    That's were I'm from.

Figure 5-4. I Am From . . . Milwaukee

I am from Milwaukee, born at St. Mary's hospital.

I am from a family celebrating the tradition of singing the "Happy Birthday" song on birthdays.

I am from the "Club Closet" and being cramped in bags, coats, backpacks, and jackets smelling that dusty irritating disgusting smell, that nasty taste of dust.

Drives me nuts.

I am from the annoying sound of me and my brother's voice.

I am from the tragic death of my Tio Christian. Seventeen shots total to the body. We still visit his grave on a few holidays.

I am from a hard working family who care.

That's where I'm from.

Identifying Genres

Genre is often a consideration when kids choose a new writing circle topic—like when the Silver Snakes decide to write "a poem about dreams or dreaming." What shape will the writing take? Anecdote, letter, poem, Facebook profile, fable, breaking news? Genre often clarifies how a piece will develop as well as its tone, voice, and style. As Lucy Calkins (1994) writes, "The forms in which we write become lenses that affect our way of seeing the world" (357). Real-world genres surround kids: morning announcement, read-alouds, comic books, text messages, stories, essays, poems. The key is becoming aware of them. What genres from their reading and writing are kids already familiar with?

Calkins (1994, 362–63) mentions three genre minilessons that help define the range of genres as well as demonstrate how significant genre choice is in writing:

1. *Define genre through what we read.* Fill a large container (a plastic laundry basket, for example) with books from the school library and identify the genre of each book as you empty the basket in the classroom: "You may want to write an alphabet book, as this author has. . . ."

2. *Model genre choice.* To help students "imagine different genres" when they write, take a collection of notebook entries on a subject and model genre choices that come to mind: "I *could* write this as a poem. . . . I could, on the other hand, write this as a letter." Then have kids work in pairs reading sample drafts and asking, "What genre possibilities do I find here?"

3. *Genre switch.* Donald Murray helped Calkins and her colleagues see how to shape and reshape material by asking them to think

about a topic in writing. "Just write whatever you want to write." Ten minutes later, Murray stopped them and asked them to reimagine what they'd written by trying a different genre. Model Murray's process, then have kids take a topic through two or three genre switches. "How would your topic develop through a letter? What would happen if you expressed your topic as a poem? What if it was a David Letterman Top Ten List?" After they've finished writing, have kids share one of their genres in small groups.

As kids write in various genres, make a genre list and display it prominently. Writing circles encourage kids to write in different genres. Genre choice necessarily involves kids in decisions about form, point of view, language, and audience. Choosing to write in a certain genre is thinking like a writer. Here's a meta-list of writing circle genres adapted from Regie Routman (1991, 171) and Nancie Atwell (1998, 492–93):

Advertisement/commercial
Anecdote
Another point of view
Biography/profile (about-the-author, resume)
Book blurb/back cover copy
Breaking news
Brochure
Cartoon and comic strip
Conversation (dialogue, text message, overheard conversation)
Crossword puzzle
Definition (encyclopedia and Wikipedia entry)
Description
Diary/journal
Essay/editorial/opinion piece
Eyewitness account
FAQs
Instruction/how-to
Interview
Letter (advice, complaint, love, Dear John, sympathy, inquiry, application, protest, apology)
Lists/notes
Memo

Discussing New Writing Ideas

Memory/memoir (six-word memoir, personal memoir, neighborhood
    sketch, family history)
Narrative
Newsletter
Obituary
Oral history
Parody/satire
Personal metaphor
Picture book
Poetry (haiku, found poem, free verse, list poem,
    song lyrics, "I Am From . . .")
Postcard
Questionnaire
Quiz
Reports (sports, weather, news)
Review (movie, restaurant, CD, live performance)
Rules/regulations/directions
Scripts (dramatic monologue, skit, one-act play)

Speeches (campaign, graduation, wedding, nomination,
   farewell, eulogy)
Stories (tall tale, science fiction, fantasy, parable, fable, fairy tale,
   mystery/suspense, love story, what if?, chain story)
Stream of consciousness
Want ad/personal ad
Web writing (email, blog, discussion board, Facebook wall, Twitter,
   Instant Message, e-zine, podcast)
Written description of a photograph

Recap

You probably have your own favorite "writeable moment" activities that
introduce kids to new ways of writing, new writing ideas. No activity is
necessarily better than any other. The point is to intentionally involve kids
in experiences that help them feel confident about drafting the writing topics they have in reserve. The ability to explore writing ideas in a relaxed,
fluid manner is essential. The bottom line is that kids need to feel comfortable drafting and need to have a list of topics to write about.

6 The Writing Circle Notebook

The writing circle notebook is a window into the writer over a short but concentrated period. Often messy but accessible, the notebook captures the full range of the writing circle adventure: drafts written; topics suggested, chosen, and addressed; genres attempted; responses given and received; reflections prompted by thinking back on each writing circle; risks, challenges, and disappointments. The physical form of the notebook varies from classroom to classroom: binder, loose-leaf folder, pocket folder, a bound journal in combination with a loose-leaf folder. The front cover is often personalized with decorations and illustrations.

First and foremost, kids' writing circle notebooks should contain *all* their writing circle drafts. In addition, the notebook holds significant artifacts and documentation of the writing circle process covered in class. These can include topic lists, reflections, and all aspects of the publishing circle (revisions, response sheets, editing work, and the final piece). Kids are responsible for maintaining and organizing their notebook. It is through the work in their notebook that kids document and assess their good-faith efforts and participation in writing circles. At the conclusion of the writing circle cycle, a writing circle notebook might include all the elements shown in the checklist in Figure 6-1.

Do you let kids take notebooks home or do they stay in the classroom? It's up to you: you know your kids. Often notebooks are kept in the classroom in the earlier grades, while students in the upper grades take full possession.

Figure 6-1. Writing Circle Notebook Checklist

_____ Letter (or memo, for older students) explaining how the notebook shows the student's good-faith participation in the writing circle process.

_____ Writing circle drafts, in chronological order.

_____ Writing circle think-back reflections, in chronological order.

_____ Publication circle documentation:

    _____ Drafts.

    _____ Role sheets:

        _____ Agent.

        _____ Illustrator.

        _____ Reviewer.

        _____ Editor.

        _____ Author.

    _____ Final published piece.

_____ Other writing circle artifacts: topic and genre lists; golden sentences; sticky note responses; found poems.

The Notebook as Accountability and Management Tool

Kids organize the materials in their notebooks at the end of writing circles or at the conclusion of the publishing circle. If good-faith effort is part of how kids' writing circle work will be assessed, a concise expression about how good faith can be observed in the collected materials serves as an appropriate introduction. It should be short and informal—a letter, a memo, or an email. How would kids describe their good-faith participation in writing circles in four or five sentences? Give kids a sense of what this might look like by modeling your own introductory statement. Kids will be reminded of what constitutes good-faith effort as you talk about the reasoning behind what you are highlighting: number of drafts written; management responsibilities undertaken (serving as first writer and timekeeper, helping the group reaching consensus); new approaches, topics, and genres tried. There will be more than enough to point to in order to show good-faith effort. Ask kids to think of this introductory piece as a frame for or window into the work to follow.

The Notebook as Writing History

The writing circle notebook is also a resource kids use to understand themselves better as writers. As students assemble and maintain their notebook, what do they notice about the language they use, the genres they employ? Minilessons about writing and writing craft take on an authentic immediacy when kids look through their notebooks to provide examples from their own writing. For example, during a minilesson on stronger verbs, kids can scan their drafts to check what kind of verbs they're using, singling out their best ones. In a minilesson on strong leads, kids might reread the opening sentences of their writing circle drafts and choose one to revise.

Rereading their writing circle notebook and looking back on this history in their notebook pages, helps kids understand the elements of good writing, the importance of voice, and the general itinerary of their writing circle travels.

Thinking Back on Writing Circles

Kids should complete a reflection after every writing circle and keep them together in one section of the notebook for easy reference. You can use a simple template to expedite and structure this reflection. A good template should reflect the definition of good writing in your classroom. It serves two purposes: documentation and guidance. Documentation includes basic information about topic, type of response, whether the response was initiated by the writer (W), the new writing circle topic, and the general degree of participation in the process. If it's important for kids to try different genres, add a place for kids to jot that down as well.

Types of reflection should be modeled and focus both on the writing completed and on group process. The reflection helps writers keep track of what happened during a writing circle meeting and reminds them of the agreed-on topic and roles for the next writing circle meeting.

Provide a blank template for each writing circle meeting. Figure 6-2 is an example of a completed think-back reflection; a blank template is shown in Figure 2-1, page 28). If you want a daily sense of how writing circles are going, you might want to collect the think-backs, read them through, and then return them to kids for safe-keeping in their notebooks.

Think-back time.

Figure 6-2. Writing Circle Think-Back

Date: *Dec. 5*   Writing circle name: *Allstars*   Writing topic: *Robots*

Name: *Julio G.*   Type of response: *One Question (W*)*

Draft ready? (*Yes*) No

Did I share my writing with the whole class? (*Yes*) No

My suggestion for today's new writing topic: *Principal for a Day*

New writing topic chosen by my writing circle: *What bugs me*

Reflection on today's writing circle:

I liked this writing better than some of the other things I've written. The questions made me think of some things I didn't think were important. Having your own personal robot would be awesome.

For the *next* writing circle meeting, I am:

First Writer: Yes/(*No*)   Timekeeper: (*Yes*)/No

Don't forget to bring a new writing topic suggestion to the next writing circle.

---

*Indicates the writer requested the "one question" response.

The Notebook Conference

Writing circle notebooks help us better understand kids as individual writers—the topics and genres they attempted, the risks they took, the craft they learned along the way. The main reason for reading through a kid's writing circle notebook isn't to grade or judge the writer, but to understand the kinds of choices he or she is making. Through their writing circle notebook, kids teach us what they've learned and accomplished.

A writing circle notebook conference focuses on where and how the writer is traveling, the kinds of language and genre choices being made, and the emerging qualities of voice. It can be held with one student at a time, with a group of two or three kids, or with an entire writing circle. Here's how you might proceed:

1. Begin by talking about three positive (and specific) things you noticed in reviewing the writing circle notebook. This can be anything from an instance of good writing (like a strong verb or an effective sentence) to observations about how the writer experimented with language, tried a new genre, or took on writing circle responsibilities.
2. Ask kids to talk about what they observe about themselves as writers based on the work in their notebook. What are their strengths as a writer? Can they point to places in their writing where they have a strong individual voice? Do they have any suggestions for improving writing circles or their writing circle experience?
3. Suggest the next step the writer can take to become a better writer—something concrete, specific, and doable. Note this next step and follow up on it during the next writing notebook conference.

Used Not Stored

The writing circle notebook is an easy and persuasive way for kids to demonstrate their participation in the process and self-assess what they have learned about writing in general and about their writing in particular. The notebook is also a rich resource for writing circle conferences and writing craft minilessons. Writing circle notebooks are to be used, not stored. To keep a writing circle notebook is to live like a writer.

From a fifth grade class:

> Dr. Bopat,
>
> If you are reading this, then I'd like to tell you a few things. One, is that As I become an adult, I look forward to becoming an author, as you are. Secondly, I wanted to tell you which pieces to read. My favorite pieces are:
>
> 1. Ms. Borden goes to math class
> 2. The attack of the GLCCML
> 3. Scarlet and Karl
>
> You'll Find these inside of my green notebook. Skarlet and karl and The GLCCML are typed and will be found with that pile. Ms. Borden goes to math class is hand-written however will be found in the pile of typed stories (on the top) The reason I am writing this is because, as you may have noticed, I'm absent. I'll be in Florida from March 5th to March 12th, so I'll miss your interview with my class. Feel free, by the way, to browse through both of my writing notebooks and kindly excuse any spelling errors!!
>
> Yours Truly,
> Justin

Dr. Bopat,

If you are reading this, then I'd like to tell you a few things. One, is that as I become an adult, I look forward to becoming an author, as you are. Secondly, I wanted to tell you which pieces to read. My favorite pieces are:

1. Ms. Borden goes to math class

2. The attack of the GLCCML

3. Scarlet and Karl

You'll find these inside of my green notebook. Scarlet and Karl and the GLCCML are typed, and will be found with that pile. Ms. Borden goes to math class is hand written, however will be found in the pile of typed stories (on the top). The reason I am writing this is because, you may have noticed, I'm absent. I'll be in Florida from March 5th to March 12th, so I'll miss your interview with my class. Feel free, by the way, to browse through both of my writing notebooks, and kindly excuse my spelling errors!!

Yours truly,
Justin

Writing Circle Minilessons

Before any writing circle session, the class as a whole zooms in on a particular skill, strategy, genre, or literary technique. These minilessons are short, strategic, teacher-directed activities that often address things that your students are struggling with or need to practice. Linda Hoyt (2000) articulates the goals of a minilesson this way: "Teach a small, learnable amount. Practice it in real contexts. Talk about what you learned and how it worked. The minilesson is about narrowing the field of vision so that you can truly see a fine point. Study it. Then, use the new understanding in a real and meaningful way" (1). One of the classic elements of minilessons is teacher modeling—demonstrating in front of kids how some task gets done or pieces gets written. In deciding which minilessons are relevant and timely, Lucy Calkins (1994) suggests that we ask ourselves, "What is the one thing I can suggest or demonstrate that might help the most?" (194). For writing circles, minilessons that "help the most" often deal with *writing topics, skills, craft,* and *smooth writing circle management.*

The time allotted to a minilesson is usually between five and fifteen minutes. Many of the ones included here require more time because kids participate in immediate application and demonstration. As Daniels and Steineke point out in *Mini-Lessons for Literature Circles* (2004), interactive minilessons in which kids and teachers work together take longer but remain "mini-*lessons*, not mini-lectures" (6).

Writing Topics, Skills, and Craft

Writing circles encourage kids to explore new topics, genres, and points of view. As you move from circle to circle within the class and later listen to whole-class sharing, note the different genres, points of view, and aspects of craft that could be the focus for a minilesson. Young writers, like adult writers, are curious and, especially in a supportive environment, enjoy trying out the new. Display a list of genres kids have used and keep adding to it. Display a list of important writing skills and craft lessons that kids have mastered as well. Enlarge the lists through minilessons. Be open to writing circles choosing aspects of writing craft, genre, and point of view for their writing topic. For instance, writing circle topics occasionally embrace an idea *with* a genre specification—like when the Silver Snakes decide to write "a poem about dreams or dreaming" for their next circle meeting.

Which minilessons to emphasize during writing circles vary from writer to writer and class to class. The new writing topics kids bring to each writing circle meeting are crucial to their success, so topic-generating minilessons are definitely in order. Writing circles also provide opportunities to introduce the concept and qualities of writing voice, audience, and the importance of precise, concrete detail.

Choosing Topics

Why

You want kids to choose writing circle topics with an eye toward possibilities. Looking at writing this way—as a possibility rather than an obstacle—goes a long way toward making kids feel like writers and think like writers.

How

Model this yourself by asking students to suggest some writing topics. As you list them, think aloud about which topics appeal to you and why. Talk about possible ways you could write about some of these ideas. Let's say one of the suggested topics is "a mistake," and you think about the time you went rafting on the Wolf River only to end up pulling what was left of the raft from the bottom of the rapids. If it strikes you that it might be interesting to write this incident as "breaking news" or a flashback or a poem or a story with a moral, share your thinking with your students.

Now ask kids who suggested topics to join you in a fishbowl discussion while the rest of the class looks on. Have your "volunteers" sit in a circle and ask them, as a group, to choose one of the topics to write about. The ensuing discussion will open up one or two topics so that kids begin to see possible ways to write about them. The goal is for everyone to agree on a single topic or to expand a topic so it includes every kid. For example, the topic "favorite sport" becomes more inclusive if it becomes "favorite physical activity" or "getting a move on." The bad news is that writing circle topic selection takes repeated modeling. The good news is students do become comfortable with reaching consensus, and what they learn changes the way they view writing topics and writing.

And Then

The key is for kids to understand that they can write about the final topic in any way they want. Topic ownership, in this instance, is inextricably connected to point of view, style, and voice. Show kids how a good topic is one on which everyone can get a handle. Everyone can find a way to write about "where I come from"; the topic "Jonas Brothers" is generally of more limited appeal.

If a circle remains unable to find a topic, they can freewrite instead. If this happens repeatedly, a topic-search conference will help.

> How does your circle reach consensus on what to write about?
> *We discuss them until all our ideas meld down to one.*
> *We see that everybody likes it.*
> *If we don't all agree, we change it.*

Replenishing Topics

Why

Writing circles flourish when there is an abundance of things to write about. In writing circles kids are continually suggesting their own topics, thinking about other kids' topics, and coming up with additional writing ideas as a group. This generates a surplus of new writing ideas to choose from.

How

Heart map. Nancie Atwell (2002) describes a powerful way to generate writing ideas modeled on a workshop by poet Georgia Heard: kids draw the shape of a heart and fill it with meaningful people, things, events, and feelings. As Atwell poetically describes it:

Questions to Help Mine Your Heart

What has stayed in your heart? What memories, moments, people, animals, objects, places, books, fears, scars, friends, siblings, parents, grandparents, teachers, other people, journeys, secrets, dreams, crushes, relationships, comforts, learning experiences? What's at the center? The edges? *What's in your heart?* (160)

Life graph. Linda Rief's positive-negative graph, on which kids quickly sketch and graph life events on a positive-negative timeline, yields an array of surprising and significant writing possibilities. Here's how Rief goes about it:

> "What are twenty-one of the best things that ever happened to you?" I ask. For ten minutes we all list.
>
> "What are seventeen of the worst things that ever happened to you?" For another ten minutes we list.
>
> "Look back at your list and star the three most positive and the three most negative things," I say. "Is anyone willing to share what you starred?"
>
> Hands shoot up. If not, I share first. After at least half the class has shared their positives and negatives, I give the students another seven minutes to add to their lists. The discussion always gives them ideas, similar things that happened to them but they forgot. . . .
>
> "Look through your list and star all those things that you feel are most significant to you for one reason or another. You might have a lot more positives than negatives, or vice versa."
>
> The students then chart their most significant positives and negatives on a graph. (1992, 48)

Life Graph Template

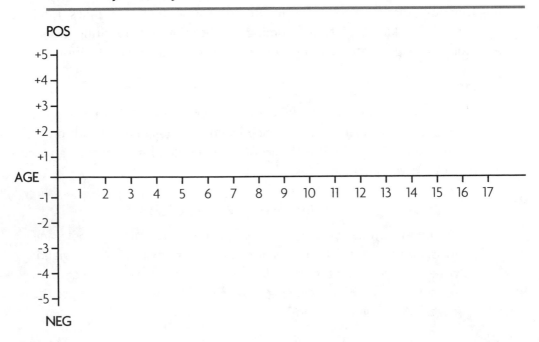

As they plot their graph, kids also provide a visual symbol for each event—like a crutch for a broken leg, a smiley face with wings for a tenth birthday party.

In creating the graph, kids not only focus on significant memories, they rank and compare them. Some kids use their actual age for the time line; others use years. A +5 to a −5 vertical line helps kids locate their memory in terms of positive or negative impact. Kids locate their incident on the time line, and then place it where it belongs on the +(positive) to −(negative) range, label and visually represent it. Once all the memories have been positioned, labeled, and illustrated, kids draw a line connecting memory to memory, starting with the first (earliest) one.

Burning questions. "Questions are the door to human wonder. Mine them with a pick ax," Stephanie Harvey writes (1998, 23). Writing circles often involve a shared inquiry—a question that so intrigues all the members of the circle that it becomes the new writing topic. *What would happen if no one died? How do camels store water? What would happen if . . . ?* Have kids make a list of four or five of their "burning questions" to share and discuss in small groups. When groups discuss the various questions, are there two or three questions that intrigue everyone in the group? When each group reports and records their burning questions, compile a list and star questions common to more than one group. Display the list and have kids sketch some flames to indicate how "burning" the questions are. Harvey suggests: "Ask students to record things they wonder on a designated bulletin board. Then have class members and school personnel check out the question board and provide information if they are able" (24).

Annotated neighborhood map. Have kids list some of the neighborhoods where they've lived. From this list, kids choose *one* neighborhood to map— just a sketch. As kids sketch, they annotate where there's something, someone, or some event that jars their memory. If, for example, they suddenly remember being chased by a dog in the alley of the apartment building across the street, they write a number (1) or a letter (A) or a symbol (*) in the appropriate spot on the map and provide an explanation in a footnote: *1. Chased by dog.* Perhaps the next memory is climbing the cottonwood tree in the back of Mrs. Cleary's house. That would be 2, B, or *: *Climbed cottonwood tree.*

Encourage kids to take a generous view of neighborhoods. As Nancy Steineke (2002) writes, "When I do this activity, I tell the kids that they can

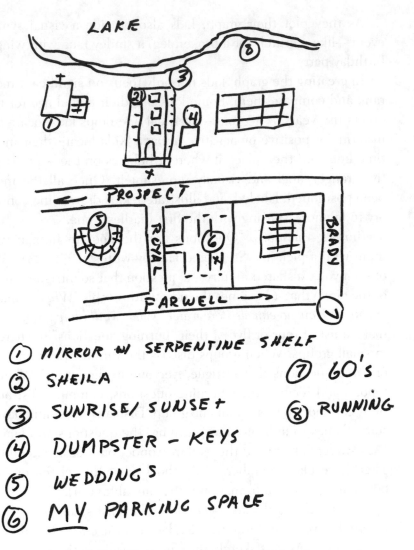

Figure 7-1. Lower east side, Milwaukee, Neighborhood Map

draw their current neighborhood, their old neighborhood, the resort where their family rents a summer cabin year after year, Girl Scout camp, any-place that represents a neighborhood to them" (2002, 115). As kids jot down their neighborhoods, make your own list on the board or a projected transparency. Choose one and as you sketch it, model how the annotations work (see the example in Figure 7-1 on page 96). Then write your own story along with the kids.

And Then

Those events, people, emotions, things that have stayed in a kid's heart; those points on a life graph; those burning questions; those people, stories, and scenarios from the neighborhood map—they're all rich, potential writing topics. Since kids are expected to bring one new writing topic to each writing circle meeting, they keep a growing list of new writing ideas at the ready in their writing circle notebooks. The stack-the-topic-deck activity (page 71) helps start this list. Topics from other writing circles, a heart map, a life graph, burning questions, and a neighborhood map can expand the list and replenish it. One characteristic of writers is that they are constantly on the lookout for interesting things to write about. By quickly reading through kids' new-topic lists, you can easily identify kids who have adopted this characteristic and those who are still struggling with finding topics that are meaningful for them and their writing circle.

Broadening Topics

Why

When kids have shared an experience, the writing circle topic is often very specific. Fourth graders at Milwaukee's Tippecanoe school who had taken a field trip to the Milwaukee Institute of Art and Design and eaten in its cafeteria were impressed by all the choices available to college art students. One of the writing circles decided to compare the cafeteria food at both places. "Our cafeteria lunch vs. lunch at MIAD" was a good writing idea; there was a shared experience to draw on, and everyone had something they were hungry to say.

But what if one kid's idea is to write about his father, a few kids like the idea, but two or three don't? Understanding how to broaden—enlarge—a topic becomes essential. You need to encourage the topic ("my dad") but broaden it so there is a writing territory in it for everyone. When the topic enlarges into "someone I admire" or "a significant person," it can include "dad" while becoming accessible to all the kids in the circle.

"Do you ever have trouble agreeing on a topic?"

"Sometimes. One day three of us wanted to write about sports and two wanted to write about special feelings and we couldn't decide."

"What happened?"

"We wrote about how a certain sport made us feel. I did skateboarding."

How

With a little help, kids quickly get the idea. Pick a particularly narrow topic—"High School Musical," "red ants," "my cat Snowball"—and have every circle quickly meet to broaden it. Help them see how "movies," "close encounter with an insect," and "favorite pet" invite more kids in.

Presenting a fishbowl discussion in which a circle chooses a new topic helps kids see the social interaction and cooperation that makes broadening a topic possible. Topic selection and achieving consensus are key to writing circle success. As you meet with different writing circles, be alert for examples of how kids do both.

And Then

When circles share their new topics for their next group meeting, note the types of topics kids are choosing and whether they seem inclusive and engaging. Proof of whether topics are inclusive and engaging resides, finally, in the writing of the kids.

Finding a Focus

Why

Sometimes it isn't a question of broadening the topic but finding a writing territory—a focus—within that topic. Once kids in a circle have agreed on a general idea to write about, they need to find their own place within that idea, a way to make that topic their own. Often it isn't the subject but what you do with it that distinguishes memorable writing.

How

Randomly select three writing ideas from the stack-the-topic deck of cards. Model the various writing options that come to your mind for the first writing topic. For the second writing topic, brainstorm options as a class. The lesson to be drawn is self-evident. Kids give other kids ideas. Often, talking about and sharing writing ideas inspires good writing. For the third topic card, have kids, in groups of three, brainstorm options and then list the results on the board or a projected transparency. Talk about the results—the repetition, the individuality, the opportunities—that present themselves when kids work together to write.

And Then

Remind kids to brainstorm different ways to write about their new topic before finishing their writing circle meeting. Make "ideas for how to write about the topic" a regular part of the writing circle rhythm.

Recognizing Voice

Why

Ever notice how kids' rough drafts can have stronger voice than the finished piece? Kids who edit their voice from their writing probably can identify voice in another kid's drafts, but have difficulty recognizing it in their own. Because writing circles give kids frequent opportunities to read their writing aloud and hear the writing of other kids, the concept of voice emerges almost intuitively, in the way one kid reads a certain part of her draft or the way a certain passage or phrase totally engages the other kids in the circle. That's because the language of writing circles is often relaxed and closer to the way kids talk. Through writing circles kids experiment with voice and recognize it in their own and other kids' writing. The goal is to get kids thinking about writing voice rather than formally defining it.

How

"I'm not sure how to define it, but I know it when I hear it" certainly applies to voice in writing. It's not that we can't isolate its qualities and elements. But when writing is read aloud (or silently), we become engaged by voice all at once. Only in retrospect do we appreciate all its parts. Voice is the unexpected turn of phrase, the earnestness of expression, the stylistic flourish meant to engage and entertain—writing with conviction and purpose. Voice is "the sense that a real person is speaking to us and cares about the message" (www.nwrel.org/assessment/scoringpractice.php). Sometimes voice is a consequence of the writer's passion for what he or she is writing about.

Pet peeves anyone? First give some examples of your own: tailgators! people who cut in line! double dippers! Before kids make their own lists, they need to understand that a pet peeve is, according to Wikipedia, "a *minor annoyance* that causes great frustration in an individual." War greatly disturbs and is too major to be a pet peeve. Corruption, death, or poverty cannot be seen as minor annoyances.

Have kids list at least four pet peeves and then share the lists in small groups of three or four kids. Kids should concentrate on asking informational questions about one another's lists. After about seven minutes, end the pet peeve discussions and have kids freewrite a five-minute draft, using their lists in any way they're helpful. Kids then return to their groups and share their writings. Group discussion should focus on where in the writing kids hear what they consider to be strong voice—like the rhythm, balance, and wit in Lindsey's survey of what really bugs her:

- I can't stand it when someone stops the microwave timer with time left especially if there is less than five seconds. Just press clear!
- I can't stand it when the dishwasher is running and someone opens it to put something in. Just wait!
- I can't stand it when someone thinks I can't do something because I am a girl. That doesn't mean we aren't physically able or that we can't catch a football or throw a Frisbee as far as a guy could.
- I can't stand it when people don't think I have intelligent opinions just because I am not an adult. Really immature behavior also bothers me. There's a time and place to act dumb and most often it's not that time.
- It really bothers me when people get emotional over stupid things.
- I can't stand not being able to finish a song if I am near the end. And I really dislike being interrupted.
- It really bothers me when people tell me to do something in the form of questions. Such as, "Do you want to do the dishes?"

In writing circles, voice is always emerging.

And Then

Take advantage of opportunities to point out examples of strong voice in read-alouds and particularly in the writing kids share in their circle and with the whole class. Follow up by giving voice to voice, so to speak. Ask kids to look through the drafts they have collected in their writing circle notebook and identify a passage where there's "the sense that a real person is speaking to us and cares about the message." Kids can first share their passage in small groups; then have each group share one of the passages with the rest of the class.

Including Detail

Why

Vivid details bring writing to life and are essential components that make a piece of writing credible. When kids' writing comes across as vague and generic, it's often because they've used vague and generic details. Memorable details, on the other hand, tend to be specific, intimate, and concrete. Showing kids the importance and nature of good details also shows them how a writer looks at the world: up close and personal.

How

Framed descriptions. Have kids cut a frame from a half sheet of cardboard or large index card. The frame can be a square, rectangle, or triangle—any geometric shape. Looking through the frames, kids examine their environment (including one another). It's similar to looking through a camera viewfinder to get just the right photo. Instead of a photo, however, kids are looking for three "shots" to describe in a couple of sentences. The frame allows kids to focus on specific visual details, and many of the resulting sentences will be precise, concrete, physical, and evocative. Then have kids choose one of their three framed descriptions to share with the whole class. Use these descriptions as the basis for a minilesson about the kinds of words that leave a physical impression—those concrete visual details that nail a sentence's credibility.

Visualization. Kids imagine what they are writing about in order to come up with the details they need to make writing credible and real—whether the topic is fiction or nonfiction. To introduce the power of visualization have kids focus on something specific—a memorable person, a favorite place, an accident, an important incident or event in their lives. Once they have something specific to focus on, help kids get comfortable and relaxed. Have them pay attention to their breathing, close their eyes, and imagine their scene, their person, their place, as you guide them: *Who is there? What do things look like? Where are you? What time of day? How does it feel? Take a photograph of the moment.* Pause between your questions and speak in a slow, meditative tone; you want kids to concentrate on what's happening inside their head, not on you. When kids open their eyes, have them jot down everything they've seen and heard and felt. Encourage lists of short phrases and single words. When lists are more or less complete, ask kids to write for ten minutes about the person, place, or event they were visualizing, incorporating any or all of the entries on their list. Then have kids listen for concrete details and images as they share their drafts with one another. When kids struggle for the right detail or image, sometimes the solution is as easy as closing their eyes and visualizing.

Listening walk. Open the classroom door and, if you have them, the windows. Eyes closed, kids all concentrate on listening. After two minutes they open their eyes and list what they have heard. Each kid shares a sound with the whole class (repetition is fine). Next, take it outside. Ask kids to pay the same attention to sound—but with their *eyes open*. Plan the walk so there's a variety of possible sounds and provide enough time—ten or fifteen minutes. Walk slowly, listen intently, no talking. After the walk, ask kids to list what they've heard. As each kid shares a detail she or he heard, compose a class poem on the board or overhead (see the example in Figure 7-2). The finished poem captures the essence of the experience: the importance of sensory detail to meaning and sentiment.

Figure 7-2. A Listening Walk Poem

Our Listening Walk

On Thursday, we went for a listening walk.
We had to be very quiet so we could hear sounds.
We heard:
Cars, birds, shoes walking, wind blowing plastic bags,
Trucks, talking, leaves blowing away, kids kicking rocks, trucks beeping,
Saws, wind, airplanes, workers putting concrete on bricks,
People walking on the grass, Mrs. Knapp's keys, Mrs. Knapp talking.

And Then

Point out good details when you hear them in small- and whole-group sharing. As kids hear other kids' details in their writing, they will start to include more in their own work. "Share your best detail" is a quick way to include everyone in whole-class sharing and underlines the importance of visualization and sense impression to good writing.

Engaging Your Audience

Why

The audience is a major component of writing circles. All kids in a writing circle share their drafts with one another, and they are generally conscious of this potential audience as they write their drafts. Many kids put effort into engaging this audience—implicitly using language and genre in new ways to entertain, surprise, and create an effect.

How

Start to make explicit the connection between language and the effect it produces by having kids write an emotion, mood, or feeling on a blank index card: *bored, anticipation, hunger, peaceful, regret, pressure*. Head kids off in advance by setting guidelines about emotions to please avoid, like wanting to punch someone. Single-word emotions/moods/feelings work best. Kids then stand or sit in a circle and pass their cards to their right for thirty or forty seconds until you tell them to stop. There might be a few backups—some kids having a card in each hand, others not having any. Quickly make adjustments so all kids have a card other than their own. On the reverse of the card they now have, kids draft something that will create in an audience the emotion/feeling/mood named on the card. Encourage kids to write in any genre, take any point of view. The only requirement is not to mention the word: the word has to be evoked through the writing. Then have kids read their drafts aloud in small groups, still not revealing the word. After they've finished reading, the other kids in the group guess what word they are trying to convey. Finally, have a whole-class discussion about how word and genre choices affect audience.

And Then

Once writing circles have hit their stride, focus one of the writing circle reflections by asking kids to think back on how their audience—the other members of their writing circle—influences their writing choices.

Management and Group Dynamics

As writing circles go forward, which aspects need more clarification, definition, demonstration, and practice? What's crucial for kids to understand and be able to do in order for writing circles to operate more productively? To rephrase Lucy Calkins, "What is the one thing I can suggest or demonstrate that will help writing circles run more smoothly?"

What a Difference a Name Makes

Why

When circles name themselves, they create an identity. The name they choose should reflect something unique about the circle members, individually and collectively. The process of choosing a circle name involves kids in a spirited collaborative writing experience dynamically similar to the process of reaching a consensus on topic selection.

How

Share some names of past and present writing groups as a way of talking about the importance of choosing the right name and the possible reasons for choosing one name over another. One of the most famous historic writing groups was the Bloomsbury group, named after the Bloomsbury area of London where many of its writers and artists lived. The 1750s Flat Hat Club at the College of William and Mary took its name from the mortarboards commonly worn by collegians of that time. Some contemporary adult writing group names are geographic (Pell City Pens), provocative (Six-Foot Ferret Writers), or purely descriptive (Saturday Writers); some are based on a pun (The Write Touch, Just Write) or other clever turn of phrase (Dreaming in Ink, Writers Unite). Choosing their writing circle name is an important decision for kids and can become a kind of touchstone for the clever and engaged writing that comes from kids working in collaboration (here's to you, Skateboarding Black Cats!).

Share names of kids' writing groups as well, and discuss what makes a good name. Above all, the name kids give their circle should be memorable and enthusiastically endorsed by all the members. Writing circles should choose a name for themselves at their first meeting because it's an important part of forming a sense of group identity. It helps build the necessary sense of community, identity, and ownership. We are the Aardvarks! We are the Aces! We are The Good, The Bad!

And Then

Refer to circles by their names. "Okay, High Flyers, what's your new writing topic for Wednesday?" "Let's hear some writing from the Mall Monkeys." Be open to rebranding. Sometimes, as kids work together and get to know one another better, they discover a more suitable name and rename their circle.

Friendliness and Support

Why

It seems self-evident that friendliness and support are necessary if kids are to work together freely and reach consensus on their writing topics. What friendliness and support look like and sound like during writing circles is perhaps less self-evident.

How

In *Reading and Writing Together: Collaborative Literacy in Action* (2002), Nancy Steineke describes a T-chart strategy easily adapted to writing circles. Kids work in pairs, one sheet of paper per pair. Kids fold the paper in half lengthwise to create two columns. At the top of the paper kids write *Friendliness and Support*, and then label the left-hand column *Looks Like* and the right-hand column *Sounds Like*. The left-hand column defines what kids look like when they are being friendly and offering support—what kind of body language an observer would see—and the right-hand column lists the words and phrases kids would say. Give kids some examples to get them started. "Looks like" might include *maintaining eye contact* and *taking turns*. "Sounds like" might include *"I'll start. I'm first writer,"* and *"Let's hear all the new topics before we decide."* As you give examples, emphasize that "looks like" refers to body language, while the "sounds like" column is for words and phrases kids say and these should be put in quotes. An item in the "looks like" column does not necessarily need to correspond with the idea across from it in the "sounds like" column. Each column is simply a list of actions or statements that convey friendliness and support. By definition, therefore, all examples should demonstrate positive behavior.

After giving your suggestions, have kids, in pairs, brainstorm additional items for both columns. After a few minutes, complete a master list as a class (see the example in Figure 7-3) by getting a response from each pair (from one column or the other, either is fine), taking care to turn any negative phrases ("you read too fast") into the positive ("be loud enough to be heard and slow enough to be understood"). Copy the T-chart ideas on the board or a projected transparency.

Figure 7-3. Aspects of Friendliness and Support

Looks Like	Sounds Like
Eye contact	"What's happening?"
Sitting close together in a circle	"I'm first writer. I'll start."
Kids take turns speaking	"Interesting. How would you write about it?"
Smiling	"Thanks."
All kids have their draft out and ready to read	"I'll go next."
Kids take notes on what they want to say to the writer	"I really liked the way you described the . . . ."
Nodding in agreement	"What kind of response do you want to your writing?"
Kids lean closer to hear every word	"Great topic. What do you guys think?"
Kids write new topic in their writing circle notebook	"Let's hear from everyone before deciding."
Waiting until the writer is finished before responding	"I" statements

And Then

The statements in the "sounds like" column become a script kids can borrow from when they want to be friendly and offer support. Of course each kid has her or his own way of expressing these things. Post the friendliness/support T-chart master list, and reinforce skills and behavior by adding to the list and starring specific skills you observe being used. Kids should also copy the master list in their writing circle notebooks. Have them star one "looks like" and one "sounds like" skill to focus on to improve their own writing circle interactions.

In my classroom I place a lot of emphasis on classroom community and spend a lot of time establishing class norms and teaching students how to interact with one another. Therefore writing circles fit right in. However, I could see this becoming an obstacle for teachers that do not do this. Many students have had little experience interacting in groups in the academic setting. It is crucial to the success of writing circles that the teacher spend time teaching students how to work in groups.
—Andrea Payan

Fishbowl It

Why

Show, don't tell is good advice for teaching as well as writing. Because writing circles involve a group dynamic, it can be difficult (and tedious) to detail all the elements that need to work together for the activity to be successful. Having kids in a writing circle demonstrate for the rest of the class how they solved a problem or "perfected" any essential aspect of writing circles helps everyone recognize how to achieve success.

How

When you want a minilesson to focus on a specific aspect of small-group dynamics, demonstrate the minilesson through a fishbowl conference. In *About the Authors* (2004), Katie Wood Ray and Lisa Cleveland describe fishbowl minilessons during which "children actually watch something happen, as if they were peering into a fishbowl" (94). Inside your fishbowl might be two or three students or an entire writing circle demonstrating the management minilesson. A writing circle that struggles with reaching consen-sus in choosing new writing topics can learn a lot by observing how another circle does it. "Okay, Soldier Boyz, into the fishbowl. Rewind and replay the discussion you had as you chose 'trapped in school' for your new writing idea."

One thing we do to start the writing circle is use the fishbowl technique to introduce how to do it and how not to do it. The teachers model in the

In the fishbowl.

center and the students watch and discuss what they see and hear. Observing how to do it and how not to do it is an interesting way to get students to talk about the kinds of behavior that are needed.
            —Tom Brown

And Then

As you observe writing circles in action, make a brief note in your own writing circle notebook when you observe something other circles can learn from. Note the group name, date, possible minilesson focus, and some details you don't want to forget when it comes time to reconstruct the experience in the fishbowl.

Practicing Consensus

Why

Because learning in schools is generally competitive rather than collaborative, many kids have little experience with understanding the concept of consensus, let alone how to achieve it. Since new writing circle topics are chosen through group consensus, minilessons in group decision making are essential.

How

Build a working definition of consensus by drawing on kids' experiences working together to get something done—the process they used in their circle to choose their name, for example. Ask kids to think back and make some notes about how they decided on their name (or reached another decision). Working in groups of four or five, kids share their notes and come to an agreement (another consensus) about what steps were necessary for them to choose a name they all liked (or make some other decision they all approved). Have one group share their steps with the whole class and write their steps on the board or a projected transparency. Subsequent groups can star repetitions and add new steps. In sharing how they chose their name, there's a good chance circles will come up with various ways of saying they brainstormed a bunch of names, disregarded the names they didn't like, and decided on one all of them liked—maybe not one each kid liked the *best*, but one they all liked well enough. Looking at the final class list of steps, suggest a consensus definition of consensus: *you give up a little something to get a lot—reach a general agreement with no substantial disagreement, with everyone included in reaching the final destination.*

And Then

You want to be sure that circle topics are being chosen by consensus—that each kid is participating in the process. It's not really consensus if the same kid's topic is always chosen for the next writing circle. It's not really consensus if the topics suggested aren't discussed or if some kids remain silent. When kids seem to be losing the spirit and definition of reaching a consensus, a fishbowl demonstration by one of the circles sets the stage for class discussion and problem solving. When it looks as if a particular writing circle is moving away from consensus and toward dictatorship, popularity contest, or acquiescence, do some problem solving with that circle in order to redefine consensus and reenergize kids' participation in the process.

Reaching Consensus

Why

Choosing writing topics might be one of the first experiences some kids have with reaching group consensus. In that case, congratulations for helping kids understand what consensus is and how to reach it. You have the thanks of future teachers who value group work. And you are helping kids understand and practice an essential life skill.

How

Enthusiasm for many topics is generated by the writing itself, but you definitely want everyone in the writing circle to feel good about the topic selected and the writing it will create. Explain to kids that topic consensus means everyone *wants* to write about the topic. Everyone doesn't have to think it's the best topic, but it needs to be one everyone can work with.

Given the short amount of time for new topic selection (thanks to the day's timekeeper), kids tend to move toward topic consensus quickly. After everyone in the circle has stated a new topic suggestion and there's been discussion and questions, a variation on the fist-to-five strategy (Fletcher 2002) can help facilitate the process. Here's how it works. Topics are restated and kids respond to the suggested topic showing a fist or a number of fingers to express their opinion:

> *Fist:* No way can I write on this topic.
> *One finger:* I'm not sure. Let's talk about it. (This is not an opportunity for kids to give you or one another the finger. The index finger is the one to use.)
> *Two fingers:* I can work with the topic, but I need more ideas.
> *Three fingers:* I like the topic.
> *Four fingers:* I like the topic and I've got some good ideas on how to write about it.
> *Five fingers:* It's a great topic, and I can't wait to get started!

You may need to quickly model what the fist/one-two-three-four-five-finger response looks and sounds like. Not all writing circle topics will

Second graders reach a consensus about their new circle topic.

garner five fingers from all the kids in the writing circle, but there should be a combination of fours and fives and not that many threes.

By definition, *consensus* means a shared agreement. Any kid in a writing circle can, in effect, block or veto any topic. Kids can really get into the idea of veto, so it's good to have some ways to head that off. Make sure kids understand the reason for vetoing a writing topic in the first place. Who wants to write about something against their will? No one. The point at which a writing topic becomes coercive is the point at which it should be abandoned. At the same time, sometimes kids reject a writing topic without really thinking about it. A knee-jerk rejection of a topic can eliminate a potentially excellent choice. One of the purposes of writing circles is to give kids experience and practice in making unfamiliar writing topics their own, to send them off into new and inviting writing territory. Be upfront with students about this goal. When a kid puts up his fist and effectively blocks a new writing topic, he has a responsibility to voice support for one of the other potential topics or offer a new or broadened topic.

That way the veto becomes part of a positive process to move the group forward to consensus.

And Then

Overused, fist-to-five runs the danger of limiting the kind of questioning and discussion that needs to take place in order to reach consensus. Maybe kids only need three signs, like thumbs up, thumbs down, and thumbs sideways. After discussing new topics, it's useful to have a strategy for seeing which topics have interest and support. Something like fist-to-five or my three thumbs isn't even an option when kids quickly gravitate toward one or two new topic suggestions. But when how kids feel about the suggested topics is hard to gauge, a way to conduct a quick opinion poll saves time and clarifies kids' choices.

Celebrating Writing as a Class

Why

After circles have shared some of their writing with the whole class, there can be an awkward silence. Silence is not a very positive response to writing, especially when kids are sharing a good day's work. Why not settle on some whole-class ways to say thank-you and celebrate the sharing?

How

Generate a list of ways to celebrate writing as a class. Ask students for examples of how we celebrate and show appreciation and delight in other areas—concerts, sporting events, bullfights. The idea is to have options for eliminating the awkward silence that sometimes descends after whole-class sharing of writing. Here are some possibilities:

- Polite applause (as at a classical concert).
- Crescendo (rising and then falling) applause.
- A shout-out (short burst of shouting and yelling, as at a sporting event).
- Finger snaps.
- The wave (started by those nearest the writer).
- Sign language applause: hold both hands in the air, palms facing out, fingers splayed, and move your wrists from right to left and back many times.

- An ovation (loud clapping and shouts of *Bravo!* and *Encore!*).
- A "round" of applause (hands moving in a circle as they clap).
- A drum roll (brief, spirited drumming on desk tops).
- A class cheer (*All right! Way to go! Olé!*).
- Hallelujah (the first few bars of the Hallelujah Chorus).
- Sandpaper kisses (rub palms of hands together and then open them up to blow a kiss in the author's direction).
- The roller coaster (palms down, hands ride the coaster—be sure to say how many hills are involved: "Stop after three hills or you'll fall off").
- A standing ovation (all kids on their feet, fingers linked together above their head in a big O).
- Thumbs up.
- W–O–W (three fingers of each hand held up on either side of an O-shaped mouth).
- Fireworks (clap hands together and wind them like a snake up over the head, where they burst apart; then wiggle the fingers like sparkles slowly falling from the sky).
- Show the love (reach out toward the author, arms outstretched, fingers moving rapidly with positive energy).
- Stomp! Stomp! Clap! Clap! (Doesn't work that well long term if the classroom is directly over the principal's office!)
- A Charlie Chaplin kick (everyone stands up, jumps in the air, and kicks his or her heels together; takes some practice).
- Eight claps in unison (because "eight is great").
- Raise the roof (palms pushing up raising the weight of the roof, accompanied by a *Woop! Woop!*).

And Then

Once you've generated a list of celebratory responses, practice and use them. Before whole-class sharing, choose one of the responses, practice it quickly, and use it to honor each writing circle after they share their work with the rest of the class. These responses might seem a little goofy, but they are fun and encouraging. They also provide an enjoyable transition between sharings. After kids have a sense of the different ways to celebrate, they can request what they want before reading their work. "*Show the Love* when we're done."

Keeping Records

Why

In writing circles kids are expected to document and keep track of their work. The writing circle notebook and think-back reflection sheets facilitate this record keeping. Making recording responsibilities clear to kids expedites this process.

How

Ask kids to list some of their accomplishments: something they've made, something they've learned how to do, a special achievement, a personal goal they've met. Ask them to share their lists in groups of three, choose one accomplishment from the three lists, and play no-you-didn't. Basically, two kids challenge the third to prove she or he accomplished what was claimed. How would you prove that you did indeed clean up your room, bake a cake, win at soccer, learn how to send email? Proof can be presented in many forms: a photo of the cleaned room, a slice of the cake, corroboration from another kid who played in the soccer game, a copy of the email you sent. As kids share their proof it becomes clear that simply saying you accomplished something isn't as convincing as producing corroborating evidence.

If good-faith effort (Chapter 11) is to be a factor in how kids' writing circle work will be assessed, list the kind of proof kids will need in order to demonstrate that effort:

- Writing drafts from each writing circle.
- Think-back reflection sheets (including whether they were first writer or timekeeper or shared with the whole class).
- New-topic lists.
- Agent, reviewer, author, illustrator, and editor sheets from the publishing circle.
- Final revised and edited writing.

And Then

Before kids complete their first reflection, model think-back on one of your writing circle experiences and share the reasoning behind the notes you make. Complete the form on a projected transparency, vocalizing your thinking as you write. Once kids are more experienced with writing circles, the members of a writing circle or individual kids can provide further mini-lessons by talking about the records they keep and how they keep them.

Additional writing circle minilessons will come to you through your observation and participation in writing circles, kids writing, and what kids have to say in their think-back reflections. When you rearrange the classroom and place a writing circle in the center for a fishbowl minilesson, take time to appreciate how powerful it is for kids to teach kids, how rich the possibilities.

Positive Response

A distinctive feature of writing circles is positive response to writing. Kids sometimes resist the unfamiliar, and unfortunately giving (let alone getting) a positive response to writing is something foreign to many of them. Writing circles expand the options kids have when they respond to one another's writing and provide numerous opportunities to practice different responses. These responses are often the focus of minilessons presented with the intention that kids will try out the specified response once they start to share their drafts.

General Principles

Writing circles support the writing of *all* students, regardless of their level of skill, wherever they are in their personal history as writers. It's an interesting way to look at kids in the classroom. What's happening now plays a role in every kid's writing future. Writing circles give kids opportunities to receive responses from someone other than the teacher and to hear a variety of responses in the "kid language" they can understand.

The writing kids share in writing circles is basically in draft form. (Remember, that doesn't mean it's not thoughtful and creative.) It's entirely appropriate that response to such writing is low-risk and supportive. The goal of improved writing self-esteem is thwarted if response becomes critical or dismissive. In an article about online writing groups for teachers, Anne Elrod (2003) says an ideal response to writing should sound "like kitchen conversation." What's the equivalent school metaphor? Lunchroom conversation? The challenge is that many kids are not sure how to have such a conversation.

Kids need to see how to give constructive responses, and unfortunately many teachers are famous for negative labeling and hurtful feedback. We don't want kids to imitate us in that regard. So we have to show and teach them. How kids respond to one another's writing needs to be defined and structured, learned and practiced, or their responses will tend to go in repetitive circles for lack of a different model.

You can define helpful and unhelpful ways of responding to writing through modeling and minilessons. Ask kids what kind of response they want from other kids when they share, and list what they come up with. Kids will most likely mention positive, supportive responses even if they phrase them as a negative ("don't make faces"). If they don't envision positive response, that's a good place to begin the conversation.

There should be opportunities in this discussion for you to help kids understand the difference between talk about the writing and talk about the writer. Instead of saying, "Your statement about the car crash confuses me," it's more helpful to say, "I'm confused about the car crash." The first response puts the writer immediately on the defensive. The latter focuses on what's happening (or not happening) in the writing for the listener, the reader, the audience—it starts a different kind of conversation. "Oh. What's confusing?"

Encourage kids to start their responses to one another's drafts with "I." "I liked the surprise ending." "I didn't understand how old your cousin is." "I" statements help focus response on what other kids in the circle are thinking and feeling about the writing.

Guidelines

Response guidelines exist to make sure the writing is heard and the writer encouraged. They will vary depending on your classroom, your grade level, and the kids in front of you this very moment. Contributing fourth-grade teacher Abigail Plummer and her students came up with these guidelines:

When Sharing Writing
Tell your circle the kind of response you want before you read your
   draft.
Read straight through with no apologies or explanations.
Read slow enough and loud enough for other kids to hear.
Listen to responses.

When Responding
Use put-ups, not put-downs.
Listen to the writer.
Take turns.
Give one response.

Cheryl Armstrong of the South Coast Writing Project uses the guidelines shown in Figure 8-1. With your students (and your colleagues, if they are using writing circles), reach a consensus (another opportunity to model that process) about your general response guidelines.

Figure 8-1. Writing Circle Writer/Responder Roles

Writer

Before you read, tell your circle the kind of response you want and/or need.

Read your words out loud; see what they sound like.

Read the piece straight through with no apologies or explanations.

Responders will stay quiet for a few moments and then begin; listen to the responses.

Responder

Your job is not to judge or to analyze, but to share your response.

A response is not an evaluation of the writing but a report of what happened to you as you listened.

Pay attention to the author's requests regarding the kind of response he or she wants.

Listen and stay quiet for a few moments after the reading ends.

Try to give a specific response to the work.

Ask whatever questions you have.

Use "I" or "what if" rather than "you should" statements.

Writing circle responses are "win-win." As Peter Elbow and Pat Belanoff observe in the third edition of *Sharing and Responding,* "the reader is always right; yet the writer is always right" (2000, 4). And it isn't really a question of right or wrong anyway. Instead it's about kids sharing what they experience while listening to the writing, and the writer listening and deciding what to do with the response, if anything. The way adults respond in professional writer's groups can provide useful models. A Mercer University Law School advanced writing group response guideline makes sense for kids' writing circles as well: "When you offer feedback in a writing group, remember that your main job is to help the writer understand what is going on in your head as you read the draft" (Edwards, 2005, 3).

> Student: "I got to share my ideas without them being put down or ignored."

To encourage the "ordinary talk" aspect of response, begin by having kids talk to each other instead of writing their response. The advantage of a spoken response is it's faster and can lead to conversation. A slight disadvantage is that one kid might just repeat what another has said because it sounds better ("I thought the same thing as Alesha"). The advantage of written response is that it involves additional writing and can be saved by the writer for future reference. The writer collects the responses, reads them through, and makes a brief comment or observation or just acknowledges the feedback. When saved by the writer, written responses become writing circle artifacts, something the writer can think back on and take forward as well.

Who Chooses?

Once kids have a good understanding of a number of different ways of responding, the writer requests the kind of response she or he wants. Kids enjoy identifying response by name: *point out*, *say back*, *sketch it*, *just the facts*. It also saves time. The writer simply states, "Point out," and starts to read the draft aloud. Other kids in the circle know to listen for something they like that they can point out when it's time to respond. Having the writer choose the type of response shifts the focus back to the writing/writer part of the writing circle dynamic. The goal of the circle is to help every kid become a better writer. What writers want to know about their writing is the most important question of all.

The writer's choice of response needs to be an informed choice, however, and it's worthwhile to teach kids how to purposefully choose from a number of options:

- *No response*. Sometimes writers aren't ready for (or don't want) any response.
- *Point out*. Sometimes they want to know what details are connecting.

- *Say back.* Are they getting their main idea across?
- *Just the facts.* How would other kids summarize their writing?
- *Sketch it.* What do other kids visualize from the writing?
- *Suggestion.* Do kids have an idea for making the writing better?
- *One question.* What do kids wonder about the writing?
- *Writer's craft.* How does the writer put words together?
- *Association.* What personal and real-life connections does the writing trigger?
- *A star and a wish.* A combination of pointing out something positive (a star) and making a suggestion (a wish).

Types of Low-Risk Responses

Kids need to know what to listen for when the writer shares a draft. Whether chosen by the writer, the circle, or the teacher, the kind of response needs to be clear before the first writer reads his or her draft aloud. The types that follow aren't exhaustive but give you a sense of some available options. Choose four or five responses that you feel will benefit your students the most, teach them through minilessons, and then have kids practice them in their writing circles. After kids are comfortable and understand different responses, writers can choose the kind of response they want from the other kids when they share their drafts.

No Response

Silence can indeed be golden as long as the writer requests it. The writer reads the draft aloud. Kids in the circle listen but do not comment except to say thanks or its equivalent when the writer is finished. Variations are to make copies and have kids in the circle read the draft silently or post the draft on the class Web space so it can be read online. Sharing with no response helps produce "an unpressured setting for getting comfortable reading your words out loud and listening to the writing of others" (Elbow and Belanoff, 2000, 7).

Minilesson. The purpose of the minilesson is for kids to realize how important it is to be able to hear their own words. Use a draft of your own writing or another short piece unfamiliar to kids. Tell kids that you want to share some writing with them, that you just want them to listen and enjoy the experience, and that you aren't going to be asking them to respond to the writing in any way when you are finished. They should "just experience the writing." Then read the writing really fast and sometimes not loud enough. When finished, ask kids to comment—not on the writing, but on the listening experience. It's obvious but needs to be restated: for reading your writing aloud to work on the most basic level of communication, it has to be able to be heard. Tell kids it's okay to interrupt the writer to say "I can't hear you," or "you're going too fast"—that it's not impolite but a sign of really listening.

Point Out

Kids *tell* the writer what words, phrases, or details stick in their mind—as when we literally point our finger at something of particular interest ("Look at the size of that hamster."). A point-out response, however, is figurative rather than literal. Also, kids learn more from success than failure, so the thing pointed out should always be positive. In other words, don't point at something you don't like when you can point at something you do like. Pointing out often starts with "I liked" or "I noticed," followed by something specific from the writing. "I noticed the colors you used to describe the picture." "I liked when you said, 'You can't live without people.'" "I noticed you used a couple of awesome comparisons." "I was surprised your dog had surgery and still weighs a hundred pounds." The writer can ask for further explanation/clarification if she wants or remain silent and simply "receive" the information.

Minilesson. Provide a fishbowl demonstration using one of the kids' drafts or a short familiar text. Have kids in the fishbowl listen to the writing, jot down one thing they notice or like, then share their responses with the group. Focus class discussion on how there's no right or wrong and that different readers are attracted by different things when they read. It's a good argument for having more than one response to writing. (Can everyone say *writing circles*?)

Say Back

Here, kids *say back* in their own words what they hear the writer getting at. "What I hear is . . . ." Say back is restating the writing's main idea, capturing the writing's essence in a simple sentence or two. What's the writer saying? "You're telling us you love to collect pins and postcards." "I think the point is some people are cool and some are mean." "I think you're getting at how football isn't only for boys." "You were sad when you heard Brett Favre was going to retire." "You love sitting and doing basically nada."

Minilesson. Read a short text aloud—some of your own writing or another unfamiliar piece. After the read-aloud, have kids jot down in their own words what they think the writer is getting at. Then ask kids, in small groups, to say back the main point of the piece. Talk about what makes this kind of response most useful: it's not judgmental, it's not an interpretation, it's not a rating, it doesn't offer an opinion. It's just a clear, direct statement of what the writer has to say about the subject:

> You love to play volleyball.
> This is what happened to two divers, when one of them got his foot
>   stuck under a rock.

Just the Facts

Joe Friday, the main character of early television's *Dragnet* series (1950–70), uttered the famous line, "Just the facts, Ma'am, all we want are the facts." Friday wanted to know details not open to interpretation or question. For this kind of response, kids have to be objective about what they hear and tell the writer what they know to be true about the writing. Succinctly. Just the facts. It's more of a summary than the say back is.

Minilesson. Work with a short text—your own draft, a read-aloud, or (with permission) one of the kids' drafts. Here's an example:

Favorite Animals

Everyone has a favorite animal. One of my favorite animals is a bird. It is because I like how birds sing with a loud voice. They fly a lot. I wonder how could they fly a lot and not be tired quickly. When I see them, I wish I could fly. One thing I don't like about the birds is that they like to eat a lot of worms. But that's their food. Finally I wonder what it feels like to fly all around above different places.

Detective Friday wanted to know *just the facts*; he wanted his informants to be objective. "I don't get why you like birds" is not a fact. What is a fact?

The writer's favorite animal is birds because she likes how they sing, she wonders how they fly so much and don't get tired, she doesn't like that birds eat "a lot" of worms. Responding with just the facts, kids state something they know to be true from the writing. "Just the facts, Ma'am, nothing but the facts" is an especially appropriate response to nonfiction and informational drafts.

Sketch It

After the writer shares a draft, other kids in the circle sketch a quick response and then take turns briefly explaining their sketch to the writer. The writer has the last word about how the writing relates or doesn't relate to the sketch. The writer keeps the sketches.

Minilesson. Explain the differences between a quick sketch and a carefully executed drawing. A sketch can use stick figures and diagrams and will by definition be incomplete and unfinished. Sketching is to drawing like freewriting is to writing. The point of a sketch is not to be artistic but to convey meaning through visual representations.

Read aloud a picture book that kids aren't familiar with and don't show them any of the illustrations. After you've finished, have them briefly sketch an image based on what they heard. When sketches are done, have a few kids to explain their sketch to the class—why they drew what they did. Stress that there's no right or wrong sketch and that each sketch has been launched because of the writing that has been read aloud. In writing circles when kids respond by sketching a "mind picture," they take turns explaining what they drew and why. Sketching is a creative way for the writer to learn what's connecting with the other kids. Many kids are surprised that their writing produces a visual image. The sketch-it activity can become a writing craft minilesson on the importance of writing with specific, concrete visual details. Without such details, kids can't create a mental picture of what they hear.

Suggestion

Kids can share an idea about what the writer might add, include, or think about. Suggestions are not requirements or commands. "What if" or "did you think about" works much better than the dreaded "why don't you" or "you should." Suggestions focus on what would make the writing better for the reader. "What if you told what happened after the surgery?"

Minilesson. Make sure kids understand that suggestions are not imperatives and often say as much about the reader as they do about the writing. What makes a suggestion helpful, and at what point does a suggestion inhibit the writer? A sports analogy may be helpful. Say you're trying to learn to play tennis. A group of your friends are watching you play, and in between sets they give you some suggestions to improve your serve. "Throw the ball higher when you serve," says one friend. "Hold the racket more firmly," says another. "Stand further back from the baseline when you serve so you don't foot fault." "Move more quickly to center court after you serve." "Put more top spin on it." After so many suggestions, in so many directions, you would be tempted to quit tennis and take up a less complicated sport. You don't want kids to feel that way about writing. There's nothing wrong with the tennis advice from your friends—it's probably correct—but it's altogether overwhelming.

Suggestions become less overwhelming if writing circles follow these guidelines:

- Make suggestions only at the writer's request.
- Phrase suggestions as questions rather than commands. "What did the house look like?" instead of "make it more visual." "Was it hard to end?" instead of "can you come up with a different ending?"
- It's up to the writer whether to follow through on a suggestion.
- Build on another kid's suggestion.

One Question

Use this response when there is a real need for clarification or more information. Kids ask only one question. "Was the snake poisonous?" "Was that your father or grandfather who gave you the watch?"

Minilesson. Establish guidelines. Are some questions more helpful to the writer than others? Is it appropriate to ask personal questions as well as questions about the writing? While "what made you write about that?" seems like a reasonable question, "do you really hate your brother that much?" might seem too personal. Encourage kids to ask questions about the writing, not the writer. Since response is limited to *one* question, the question should prompt the writer to think about the writing. A question that's important to one kid is not necessarily important to another. A reader's question should be about something intriguing or puzzling and be prompted by a sense of mystery and curiosity. Questions seeking more information and clarification help writers visualize and add more details.

Writer's Craft

Kids can also reinforce specific writing craft lessons in their responses by focusing on the way the writer puts words together. Descriptive words, powerful verbs, effective leads, memorable images, a sentence to remember—whatever aspect of writing craft you are teaching can be the focus for the day's writing circle response. "Okay, today in your circles, point out some active, powerful verbs in what you hear." Promote kids' interest in genre the same way: "What kinds of genre choices are each of you making in your circle writing today? Timekeepers record a list from your circle to share. We're going to start a genre bank from which you can withdraw ideas." (Also see Chapter 5.)

Minilesson. Show kids how they can learn the craft of writing from what they have written and are writing. Start by reading aloud the opening lines from a selection of favorite classroom read-alouds or the opening lines of books by a favorite author. Talk about the importance of leads as kids join in categorizing the leads you've read aloud. In pairs, kids then look back through their writing circle drafts (conveniently available in their writing circle notebook) and categorize how they start their drafts. Kids choose one of their opening lines and craft three new leads—sharing one new lead with the whole class. Crafting a new lead encourages kids to view prior drafts not as separate entities but as part of a continuum—as Ralph Fletcher (1996) puts it, "breathing in, breathing out."

Association

This response should be a nonjudgmental free association. "Your writing makes me think about hot chocolate on a cold day . . . a new start . . . my best friend Sammie . . . my puppies Duke and Ella . . . a fairy tale." The first association that comes to mind is usually a safe one (with the caveat that the association should not place the writing or writer in a negative light).

Minilesson. Read aloud a picture book that you know will appeal to all kids, something like *Wilfrid Gordon McDonald Partridge*, written by Mem Fox and illustrated by Julie Vivas. After you've finished, each kid in the class shares one thing the book made her or him think about. Some kids will connect with the illustrations, some with other books they've read, some will associate with grandparents, some will talk about their own collections and their own memories. Help kids understand that association often connects the writing to their life experiences and worldview.

A Star and a Wish

This is a favorite response with younger kids. The star is something in the writing they like. The wish is what they wish was there—usually more information about something mentioned in the writing.

Minilesson. Provide a fishbowl demonstration. Invite a writing circle to the center of the room and have one kid read his draft. When he finishes, have the other kids in the circle take turns identifying a star (similar to pointing out something they like). On the second go-round, everyone states a wish. The writer notes the stars and wishes and later decides whether to follow up on the wishes and apply the responses to their writing.

Classroom Examples

We chose a short text or student draft to demonstrate the different and distinct kinds of information each response elicits. Although all these responses would never be elicited at once in any writing circle, it's often surprising for kids to see how the response they ask for can determine the kind of feedback their writing receives (as in the draft shown in Figure 8-2).

Figure 8-2. Darkness, a Student Writing Sample

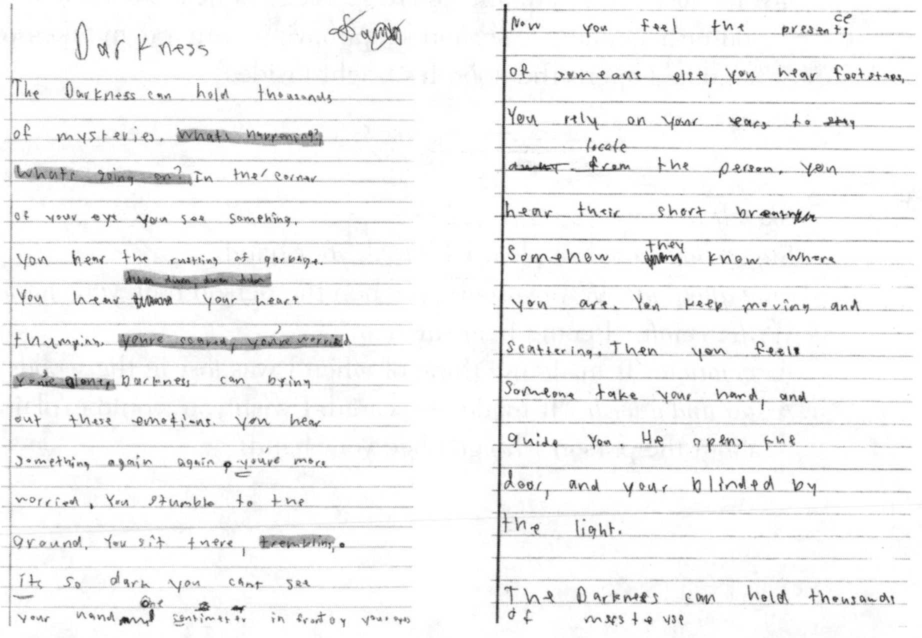

Figure 8-2. Darkness, a Student Writing Sample, cont.

Darkness

The darkness can hold thousands of mysteries. What's happening? What's going on? In the corner of your eye you see something. You hear the rustling of garbage. You hear your heart thumping, dum dum, dum dum. You're scared, you're worried, you're alone. Darkness can bring out these emotions. You hear something again. Again. You're more worried. You stumble to the ground. You sit there, trembling. It's so dark you can't see your hand one centimeter in front of your eyes. Now you feel the presence of someone else, you hear footsteps. You rely on your ears to locate the person. You hear their short breaths. Somehow they know where you are. You keep moving and scattering. Then you feel someone take your hand, and guide you. He opens the door, and you're blinded by the light.

The darkness can hold thousands of mysteries.

Responding to this draft in the ways we've just discussed shows the range of possibilities:

No response: silent appreciation.

Point out: "I like the 'dum, dum, dum dum.'"

Say back: "Darkness can hold thousands of mysteries."

Just the facts: "It's dark and you're scared. You hear someone and then you hear someone else. You keep moving until a man takes your hand and opens the door. It's bright inside."

Sketch it:

Suggestion: "I'm not clear who took your hand?"

One question: "Were you afraid when the person took your hand?"

Writer's craft: "I could hear the fear."

Association: "It made me think of when I was lost in the woods."

A star and a wish: "It made *me* scared. I wish you would explain more about the person who grabbed your hand."

When kids learn different ways of responding to one another's writing, they also learn how to become better writers. Many of these response strategies are writing strategies as well. **Point out** teaches the writer the importance of specific concrete detail; **sketch it** shows the writer the importance of visual image; **suggestion** emphasizes the importance of audience; **asking questions** helps writers realize the importance of asking themselves informational questions as they write.

Documenting Response

To help kids keep track of the different types of response, display or hand out a list of ways of responding for easy reference (see Figure 8-3). The goal is for kids to request the type of response that will be most helpful to them.

If the whole class has practiced one response, everyone writes that type of response on the daily think-back reflection template (see the example in Chapter 2, on page 28). If the writer has chosen the response, kids put a *W* (for writer) after the type of response.

Positive Response

Point Out
One thing I noticed that I liked was . . .

Say Back
I think your main idea is . . .

Just the Facts
I hear you making the following points . . .

Sketch It
As you read your draft, the picture in my mind was . . .

Suggestion
What if you . . .

One Question
What I really want to know is . . .

Writer's Craft
One thing I notice about the words you use in your writing is . . .

Association
Your writing made me think about . . .

A star and a wish
I really like . . .
I wish that. . . .

Writing Circles by Jim Vopat (Heinemann: Portsmouth, NH); © 2009

9

Enjoyable Ways Kids Can Share Writing with the Whole Class

Whole-class sharing of some writing from each writing circle builds accountability, expands kids' sense of possible topics and ways to write, and provides a window into the work of all the writing circles in the class. Often just a part of a draft is shared; the goal is to give every kid in the classroom the feeling of pride that accompanies a successful writing experience.

At the conclusion of their writing circles, kids decide as a group what writing to share with the whole class. Similar to fine-tuning the ways of responding to writing, the options for whole-class sharing need to be modeled and practiced. The sharing takes place between the end of the writing circle meeting and the day's writing circle think-back reflection, often in conjunction with individual writing circles' announcement of their new writing topic.

In general, whole-class sharing has the following rhythm:

1. The timekeeper states the circle's name and announces the new writing topic.
2. Members of the circle briefly share (for one or two minutes) some of their writing.
3. The rest of the class give a celebratory response (sandpaper kisses, show the love, finger snaps) (see Chapter 7).

The writing kids select to share with the whole class usually hasn't been revised and edited. It's writing individual kids choose as representative, or their writing circle buddies feel other kids in the class should hear. It can include a selection (a paragraph, a sentence, a memorable word or image) from everyone in the circle or feature longer parts of one or two kids' drafts or perhaps a collaboration.

Allowing one or two minutes per group, whole-class sharing takes about ten minutes. This time constraint needs to be factored in when deciding who will share with the rest of the class and how. Once kids are familiar with the various ways they can share their writing whole class (discussed in this chapter), they'll come up with some ideas of their own. In any event, you don't want to always be The Person Who Decides How Writing Circles Will Share. As kids become comfortable *within* writing circles, they become increasingly responsible for deciding how they will share their writing with the whole class.

Ways of Inviting Whole-Class Sharing

Nominations

"Madam Chairperson, The Good, The Bad nominate . . . ." Each writing circle decides, by consensus, whose draft (or part of a draft) should be heard by the rest of the kids in the class. Kids who are nominated feel confident because they know their writing circle stands behind them. We discourage circles from nominating the same candidate over and over. "Let's hear some new and exciting voices from the writing circles today."

A nominee shares his writing, flanked by members of his circle.

Let Your Light Shine

Every kid from each writing circle shares a brief highlight from her or his writing—a memorable image, a key phrase, a title, an opening or closing line. Since every kid in the class is going to share, save the celebration until the end. Someone from one circle starts off, shares, then chooses a kid from a different circle to go next. This system continues Ping-Pong style, until everyone has had a turn in the spotlight.

I Hear a Symphony

This is a random approach, but repetition gives it shape. Again, everyone in the class shares a phrase, short sentence, image, detail, or important word but this time in no prescribed order. Kids jump in when the time seems right. For this spontaneous "symphony of words" to be effective, kids need to be very aware of taking turns and not talking over someone else. They can read more than once if they have something that seems to provide continuity or contrast.

This approach to sharing is easier said than done, and you might want to play an excerpt from a symphonic musical composition and talk about how the various instruments blend together, repeat melodies or motifs, change tempos, and increase (crescendo) and decrease (diminuendo) in volume. Encourage kids to think not only of the meaning of what they've chosen to share but what it sounds like. A sharing symphony becomes more manageable if you form mini-symphonies of nine or ten kids. Takes rehearsals, but worth it.

Post It

Sticky notes come in all sizes and colors, and professional articles have been written about their versatility and effectiveness as a learning tool. Give sticky notes to all the kids. Have them reread their draft, focusing on something specific: their three strongest verbs, a one-sentence summary, their best visual detail, their title, their favorite part. Have them jot down their response on the sticky note and adhere their note on a designated chart or section of a bulletin board—which instantly becomes *must reading*. Must reading because the notes provide a class-wide self assessment as well as the foundation for real-time minilessons.

Sticky notes can also easily become part of the writing circle reflection process. Pose a good question to kids about their writing—*What genre do you want to try? From what you heard in your writing circle today, what makes good writing? What do you enjoy the most about your own writing? What do you enjoy the most about the writing of the other kids in your writing circle?* Ask students to jot down their response and post the sticky note on the board. There's no need for kids to sign their notes—we're primarily interested in the content of the notes, not who wrote them. These posted sticky notes serve as the basis for class discussion and they also become a great source of ideas for minilessons.

Open Mike

Kids sign up in advance to read all or part of their writing over an amplifier system—a kind of classroom cabaret. Even if the system isn't live, the microphone is still a good prop.

> Writing circles have been meeting every Friday. We started having an "open mike" at the end of every session, and the kids love sharing their writing this way. I need to focus them a little more on important topics and get them to be better at responding to one another's writing, but they love getting to choose the writing they do and read parts of it in front of everyone. Friday is their favorite day of the week!
> —Melissa Schmidt

Gallery Walk

Kids "hang" their writing on the classroom walls like artwork in a gallery (impose a one-page limit). They can highlight a section that expresses the essence of the piece or a particularly impressive passage or the concluding paragraph. They don't need to recopy the draft, just use a highlighter on the original. Ask them to be careful not to crowd other students' work. Once the show is up, kids can walk through the gallery, taking in (i.e., reading) the art.

Golden Sentence

A golden sentence is a glimpse into each kid's writing style and voice—a sentence that stands out because of a striking image or detail, an unexpected verb, or powerful phrasing. It's the kind of sentence you underline when reading because it affects you somehow. Perhaps students find a possibility or two as they read through their draft. Maybe they find a sentence that *could* be golden; it doesn't quite yet shine but the clouds could clear. Kids who read through their writing and don't find any gold can craft a new sentence to burnish.

Golden sentences can be posted for a gallery walk. Or have kids copy their sentence in the center of a sheet of paper and then pass it to the others in their writing circle, each kid writing a brief positive response in the blank space around the sentence. Golden sentences are not only a quick classwide celebration of good writing but also a continuing resource for teaching what constitutes an effective sentence. *Going for the gold, unlike the Olympic image it brings to mind, is noncompetitive.* Even though kids in any given writing circle are at different places in their writing development and competence, by crafting and sharing her or his best sentence, each kid in the class becomes a gold medalist.

Writing about "summer vacation," the Femme Lattes' golden sentences convey their individual point of view, writing style, and voice:

- "Strawberry, blueberry, banana frappuccino: the cold sensations collide as I sip the delicious drink."
- "The sunlight's sparkle on the lake creates a glistening mirror effect."
- "I looked out my window only to see green hills and a dark castle looming in the distance."
- "The elegant fragrance of Dove Shampoo is classy, yet modern and new."
- "It was a sunglasses day, and I loved it."

Read-Around

Each kid in the class reads aloud something specific from that day's writing circle draft. Kids could share a golden sentence or some words or phrases that demonstrate the day's writing craft minilesson. For example, if kids have been working on writing an effective lead, they can each read aloud the opening sentence of their draft. If the focus is on choosing a telling visual detail, the read-around would feature the best visual detail from each kid's writing.

Found Poem

Champions of found poetry believe poetry is waiting to be discovered everywhere—in newspaper headlines, recipes, letters, emails, instant messages, commercials, textbooks, dictionaries. There's even a Web site featuring found poems in the speeches of former defense secretary Donald Rumsfeld. Kids delight in finding unexpected combinations and arranging these "finds"—images, words, details—into a free-verse poem without changing or adding anything. (It's okay for words and phrases to repeat.)

Here's how it works. The members of a writing circle reread their draft and highlight a couple of effective words or details or a significant phrase. They copy each selection on a separate index card or sticky note. Then, as a group, they pool the cards or notes and move them around until they have created a found poem. Remind kids they can only use the words and phrases on the index cards—no extra words. Found poems from each writing circle can be displayed (another gallery walk) and/or read aloud, a collaborative demonstration of each writing circle in action.

After sharing their drafts on the topic of "my invention," the Sloths found this poem in their writings (contributions from each member are indicated by the initial letter of their first name in parentheses):

There Would Be Laws

A big box (L) you step into and turn on (K)
Red on bottom and glass on top (N)
This machine would acknowledge any language (T)
The engine (J) would use saltwater instead of gas (L)
Uploaded (K)—no one would die before they were ready (A).

First Impression/Final Impression

This variation of the *golden sentence* helps kids understand the importance of the first and last sentence in any writing. For *first impressions* kids from each writing circle share a title or first line from their draft with the whole class. For *final impressions*, kids read the concluding line from their draft.

Sandpaper kisses, anyone?

10

Publishing Circles

Writing circles become publishing circles when their purpose shifts from generating drafts to preparing a more fully developed, final piece. "No writing is ever finished," Elaine Maimon observes in *What Makes Writing Good,* "it is merely abandoned, sometimes to public notice" (1985, 337).

The goal of publishing circles is to support authors as they take their writing public. Writing circle drafts are "starts" or "probes" for longer, more formal pieces. Therefore, after approximately seven to ten writing circle meetings, kids reread their drafts looking for something they want to write and think more about. That many drafts may seem like a lot, but kids build fluency and confidence with their writing the more they work with it.

There are many advantages to having kids select one of their writing circle drafts to revisit, revise, edit, and publish. Publishing is a motivation for and celebration of writing circles and the work done in them. Publishing gives kids further opportunity to look back and reflect on their writing circle experiences, their writing, and the qualities of good writing.

Like publishing in the real world, publishing in the classroom can be an intricate process—conferring, revising, editing, formatting, going public—often taking more time than expected. When the focus changes from writing about a common topic to moving a selection forward through revision, editing, and publishing, writing circles are referred to as publishing circles to acknowledge the shift. In keeping with this shift, we refer to kids as *authors*. The names of the circles remain the same; their focus is now on making one another's writing better.

Publishing Roles

Writing circles easily become enthusiastic publishing circles. Kids are already comfortable working together and are already familiar with one another's writing. If some kids, for whatever reason, want to change circles, the transition from writing circles to publishing circles is the time to do it.

The goal is to make publishing circles comfortable and productive for everyone.

One way of structuring the publishing circle is to adapt some roles encountered in professional publishing:

- *Agent*. Advocates for the writing and the writer.
- *Illustrator*. Helps the author depict the message visually.
- *Reviewer*. Suggests revisions.
- *Editor*. Focuses on correctness.
- *Author*. Knows what he or she wants to say and is open to the best way to say it.

Providing role sheets for each "job" expedites the process. The problem with "role sheets" in general is their tendency to become mechanical. They have an initial advantage, however, in helping kids view writing through different eyes, for different purposes. Publishing involves a number of people working together, and viewing writing through prescribed points of view expands most kids' definitions of writing, writer, and response.

Schedule

Authors know that nothing is certain but death, taxes, and deadlines. Here's a quick overview (more details to follow) of what a schedule for publishing circles might look like.

Meeting 1: Choosing the Kernel

Kids spend fifteen or twenty minutes looking through their drafts in order to choose some writing they want to continue to think about and write about. Model this by searching through your own drafts for a kernel you want to develop. Think aloud about the kinds of decisions you make as you review your drafts. "I'm glad I wrote about my best friend Becky who died, but it's so personal I think I'll pass on it for now. . . . But there is this description of throwing my keys away with the garbage into the dumpster. Humorous writing is tough, but it's something I haven't tried in a while. I'm already thinking of different ways to do it. I'm going to go with that."

Once kids have chosen what they want to continue working on, they share the writing kernel with the other kids in the publishing circle and discuss their next step. Will they develop and expand it? Look at the topic from a different point of view? Just start writing more and see what happens? At the end of the meeting, kids reconvene as a whole class, each one stating the idea or topic he or she has chosen to develop.

> I asked my fourth-hour class, "Why did you pick the piece you selected to publish?" Six of them said they wanted to put more effort into it. Five wanted to make it more descriptive/detailed. Three said they liked it the best. Four were interested in the topic. Four said the other members of their circle liked it.
> —Joan LoPresti

Meeting 2: Agent Conference

Whether kids revise their writing during writing workshop, at home, or both, every kid brings a "new and improved" draft to the second meeting of the publishing circle. (Remind kids not to lose their various drafts; they are part of the documentation of their good-faith effort.) Now, in a conversation with their "agent," authors talk about their motivation (why they chose to work more on this idea) and their audience. The agent also gives the author specific information about what's working.

Before this meeting present a minilesson about "real life" literary agents—how they advocate for authors and receive a percentage of what the authors are paid for publication (usually between 10 and 20 percent). Model this advocacy by pointing out some writing you strongly feel should gain a wider audience. This can be an already published story or picture book, but it's better if it's unpublished material—perhaps a student's draft. Read the writing aloud, and then become an advocate. Tell kids why you've chosen this piece of writing to recommend, and share the reasons behind your recommendation. That's one of the jobs of an agent: *to know why the writing deserves a larger audience.*

Often in their publications kids include a brief "about the author" statement—like the short biographical sketch that appears on the back cover or last page of professional publications. If kids are going to include an "about the author" statement as part of the publication, define this for kids and give them some examples that combine some personal information while also pointing to something specific and positive in the writing. Brief and specific: "Colin McNulty moved to Milwaukee from Texas with his family when he was ten. This is the first time he has written about that experience." "Brittany Ware has written about Brewster before, but here she imagines what Brewster would say if the puppy could talk."

Each author has a ten- to fifteen-minute agent conference (documented by a completed role sheet) with *at least* one other kid in the publishing circle. Each kid should also have at least one opportunity to be an agent (and complete the role sheet). The agent answers the questions on the role sheet and gives the sheet to the author. The author reads the sheet and asks questions or reacts. Kids tend to want to see the written sheets as final, so make the point that the sheets are *the basis for a conversation*. Agents *talk* to authors. After the agent conference, authors continue to work on their writing in preparation for the third publishing circle meeting.

Meeting 3: Illustrator Conference

Kids have already had some experience with visualization and design through the sketch-it response (see Chapter 8, page 124). Again, each author needs at least one illustrator conference, and each author serves as illustrator at least once. In the related minilesson, be sure to define *illustration* broadly so that the illustrator conference *encourages imaginative possibilities*. The illustrator encourages the author to think about the visual aspects of the writing, and the author keeps the role sheet the illustrator has completed.

Remind kids that the idea is not just to prepare a sketch and pass it on but to have a conversation about the options for presenting the writing visually. The author decides what, if anything, they want to use from the illustrator's response. The point of the conference is to get the author thinking visually.

Meeting 4: Reviewers Conference

By now authors have done a lot of thinking about their piece and started some revisions. Reviewers answer the main question the author has about the piece and ask their own, in the process making more detailed suggestions for improving the writing. Each author receives at least two reviews and reviews the writings of at least two other members of their publishing circle.

Authors bring the original and a photocopy of their writing to this conference so each reviewer can read the piece at the same time. After the reviewers complete their comments and return them to the author, the author reads the comments and asks informational and clarification questions. It is up to the author how she or he responds to the reviewers' questions and suggestions. The author keeps the reviewers' role sheets and starts the final revisions.

Before this meeting, model a review conference for the whole class. Work with a draft everyone in the class can read (make a copy for everyone or project a transparency of the draft), and have the author formulate an author's question in advance. Read the draft aloud all the way through before completing the role sheet, sharing your thinking as you jot down your responses and questions. Talk to kids about their suggestions or comments; they should be encouraging, specific, and relevant.

Meeting 5: Editors Conference

Once authors have completely revised their writing and have a word-processed final copy, they are ready to confer with at least two editors. (Each author also serves as an editor for at least two other authors in their circle.) Word processing the writing makes the final editing changes easier and avoids unnecessary recopying. Before the meeting, model editorial comments and markings for the whole class, verbalizing your thoughts as you go along. Read through the entire paper first before going back to concentrate on issues of correctness.

After editors have finished their work, they confer with the author to clarify their markings and answer questions. The authors then make the editorial corrections that make sense to them and ready their piece for final publication. Final publication options can range from public display (perhaps in a gallery walk), read-aloud (perhaps at a parent celebration), as part of a collection of other finished pieces (circle or whole class), or online posting.

Do the Math

Preview the publishing circle roles and schedule with kids. Describe and explain the progression of activities (editing comes after revision, not before, for example) and kids' basic responsibilities. These responsibilities include:

1. Completing role sheets for other authors in their publishing circle.
2. Collecting and keeping the role sheets other kids in their circle have filled out in relation to their writing.
3. Exploring and developing their ideas through a series of drafts.

Although the publishing circle consists of five distinct activities (choosing the kernel and then participating in agent, illustrator, reviewer, and editor conferences), it's crucial that kids have enough time between scheduled circle meetings to work on their drafts. Whether they do so during writing workshop or as homework varies from classroom to classroom. In between circle meetings, kids are expected to write, revise, and consider the comments/suggestions of other members of their publishing circle.

Doing the publishing circle math, each author will receive responses from at least one agent, one illustrator, two reviewers, and two editors. Each publishing circle member will complete at least one agent response, one illustrator response, two reviews, two editing responses, and their own author self-reflection. The author collects the role sheets and includes them as part of the publishing circle documentation.

Role Descriptions and Forms*

Agent

In professional publishing, agents contact publishers on behalf of authors. It is the advocacy part of the agent's role, not the politics, that makes for such an interesting perspective. Kids who can advocate for the good qualities in another kid's writing are on their way to advocating for themselves as a writer as well. They are on their way to being stronger writers.

In the agent conference, the agent and the author discuss why other kids will want to read the writing and why it should be published. What's important about this writing? The way it's written? The subject matter? Why will other kids want to read it? Who's the audience? The agent's job is to advocate for the author and the writing. The agent thinks about the author's career as well. What has the writer already written and what does the writer want to write about next? How does this writing connect with the history and future of the author?

If you want agents to write their own back of the book blurb for the writing they represent, share some from the classroom library and point out the main criteria (two or three sentences, general sense of subject, and major

---

*Adapt these roles to reflect the realities of writing in your classroom.

Agent's Role Sheet

Your Name _____   Your Writing Circle _____

Author's Name _____   Writing Title _____

Sometimes editors and publishers don't "get it" until the author's agent points out the positive points about the author's writing. You are the agent. Your job is to talk with the author about his/her writing so you understand it better. Make some notes after each question/observation to give the author when done.

QUESTIONS/OBSERVATIONS

1. Read the writing or have the author read it aloud to you. When finished, tell the author what you liked. List two or three things:

2. Ask the author what he/she likes best about this writing, and write the answer here:

3. What's next for the author? Make a note of his/her future writing plans.

4. As an agent, you try to convince people to read your author's work. Write a blurb— the kind on the back of a book that is written to grab the attention of potential readers. What would you say to people who haven't read the writing to get them interested in it?

5. Help the author formulate an "about the author" statement and write it here:

Give these notes to the author and talk about your responses and observations. The author will keep your response.

---

attractions for the potential reader). Here's Myla Goldberg's blurb from the back of a book by Mark Haddon: "*The Curious Incident of the Dog in the Night-Time* brims with imagination, empathy, and vision—plus it's a lot of fun to read."

If an "about the author" statement is to be included in the publication, the agent helps the author formulate it: " 'Windy Night' is Tamara Ward's first poem. She lives with her mother and three brothers near Wrigley Field." An agent's role sheet is included in Figure 10-1 on the previous page.

Illustrator

Visualizing helps the author make the writing more detailed and concrete. When you visualize, you re-see specifics—many of which can be incorporated during revision. Increasingly, professional fiction, nonfiction, essays, memoirs, poems, and, of course, blogs, wikis, and Web sites are illustrated. Revisit illustrated writing students have already read and point out the importance of the visual image to overall meaning and audience appeal—how visuals complicate and deepen the message in the writing. How the way published writing looks can help get the message across.

Discuss the definition of *illustration* with kids. Note that it can include simple sketches, photos, collages, reproductions, symbols, cartoons, designs, graphs, artifacts, meaningful formatting, and spacing. What could make the writing "pleasing to the eye" (in the words of the 6 + 1 Writing Trait rubric)? The idea is to encourage the author to talk about visual possibilities that he or she might or might not ultimately include in the final publication. The illustrator is a design consultant and creative visionary.

The job of the illustrator is to encourage the author to think about the visual aspects of the final publication. What are the author's ideas about how the writing will look when it's published? Typeface and spacing? Placement of title and author's name? Will there be an "about the author" statement? Where will it appear and how will it be separated from the text? What are the author's ideas about "presentation" (the +1 in the 6 + 1 Writing Trait model)? An illustrator's role sheet is included in Figure 10-2.

The decision whether or not to include visuals in the final publication is up to the author.

Illustrator's Role Sheet

Your Name _____ Your Writing Circle _____

Author's Name _____ Writing Title _____

You are the illustrator. Your job is to help the author picture aspects of the writing. During a conference with the author, jot down notes to the following questions:

1. Has the author used drawings or illustrations before? Any examples?

2. What ideas does the author have for illustrating and/or formatting this writing?

3. Sketch your response to the author's writing on the back of this page. Sketch anything about the writing you liked, or sketch a suggested layout, design, or cover for the publication. When you show your sketch to the author, tell something about it: why this sketch?

The author keeps this response and sketch.

Reviewer

Each publishing circle member completes two reviews and receives two reviews of their writing. Reviewers advise the author about how to make the writing better—they provide support and suggestions. They try to keep in mind the big picture (what the author wants to say) as well as details of language. They can also point out "special words" that seem to be important or particularly effective.

The author shares in advance an important question he or she needs answered: *Any ideas for a better title? How can I make it more exciting?* The reviewer's advice can range from the specific to the general, from *Put in more details at the start* to *I was confused about who was driving the car. Can you make that clearer?* to *Don't change a thing.* The reviewer reads the writing through twice. The first time, to get a sense of the whole piece; the second time to jot down responses on the reviewer role sheet. All revision decisions are up to the author. A reviewer's role sheet is included in Figure 10-3.

Editor

Editors are concerned with clarity of meaning, punctuation, grammar, or readability. The editor makes informed suggestions about how the writing can be more publicly "correct." The editor does not make suggestions about adding or deleting language unless something is unclear. It's useful to have at least two editors for each author. This means that the author needs to make two copies of the writing available for editing. Editing happens *after* the author has made all revisions and the writing is considered "final."

Editors' underlines, circles, and marks in the margin are certain to spark discussion, because peer-editors can be mistaken. In that case, the editor also learns something. The author confers with the editors about any suggestions the author doesn't understand. Irreconcilable differences go to the publisher (you or a team of editing experts).

Whether to apply suggested corrections to the writing is up to the author. If, for example, an editor checks an incomplete sentence and the author purposely wrote it that way, the author wouldn't change it. If a word is circled as misspelled by the editor, however, the author is obligated to check out the correct spelling and make the necessary changes if the editor is right. If the editor is mistaken, the author shows the editor that the original spelling is correct. An editor's role sheet is included in Figure 10-4.

Reviewer's Role Sheet

Your Name _____   Your Writing Circle _____

Author's Name _____   Writing Title _____

You are the reviewer. Your jobs are (1) to read the writing to get a sense of its meaning, and (2) to reread the writing in order to answer the author's question and give good advice on how to make the writing even better. As you reread, jot down responses to the following:

1. What's your favorite part of the writing? What do you like about it?

2. What are some important and interesting words in this writing? What words hold special meaning?

3. The author's question is something the author wants advice about. The author writes the question here:

   Your answer:

4. Write down something that you wondered about as you reread this writing:

5. What advice do you have for the author as they revise this writing?

Give your review to the author when you have finished. The author will read through what you have written and then talk with you about it.

Editor's Role Sheet

Your Name _____   Your Writing Circle _____

Author's Name _____   Writing Title _____

You are the *editor*. Your job is to help the author make the writing as correct and presentable as possible.

1. Read the writing all the way through.

2. State something positive about the author's editing skills. For example: "You definitely know how to use capitals at the beginning of sentences."

3. *Reread* the writing, underlining words you *think* are misspelled and circling words you *know* are misspelled.

4. Put an X in the margin where the writing confuses you.

5. Put an asterisk (*) in the margin if there's a punctuation problem—e.g., periods, quotation marks, commas. If there's more than one, add additional asterisks: 2 problems = **.

Once you have edited the writing, return it and this sheet to the author. The author will read over your suggested corrections and ask questions about things he/she doesn't understand. Final editing decisions are up to the author.

Author's Role Sheet

Your Name _____ Your Writing Circle _____

Writing Title _____

As the *author* your job is to think about your writing by completing these statements:

1. The writing is important to me because:

2. Read through your writing, pick out the "golden sentence" (your "best" sentence, the one you are proudest of), and write it here:

3. The illustrator helped me:

4. The agent helped me:

5. The reviewers helped me:

6. The editors helped me:

7. One thing I learned about my writing from being in the publishing circle is:

Keep this role sheet with the agent's, illustrator's, reviewers', and editors' role sheets and the copies of your writing marked by your editors.

Author

Authors accept suggestions that strengthen and clarify their writing and pleasantly disregard suggestions they don't like. The author is responsible for collecting role sheets from the other members of the publishing circle (along with the marked copies from the editors). The comment sheets can provide a basis for an author's think-back at the conclusion of the publishing process. The author also chooses a "golden sentence"—a sentence that stands out because it creates a striking image, uses unexpected language, or makes a powerful statement. An author's role sheet is included in Figure 10-5.

Publication and Celebration

Celebrate all the hard work by publicly displaying the writing or printing copies of a class anthology of the best writing of every kid. Classroom expectations will be high. During the writing circle meetings, kids will have heard all or parts of many of the published pieces at various stages of draft and revision and will be eager to see how they came out.

Publishing circles encourage and motivate—and kids rise to the occasion. Compare the first draft and final copy of "The Air," as shown in Figures 10-6 and 10-7.

Figure 10-6. Handwritten Initial Draft of "The Air"

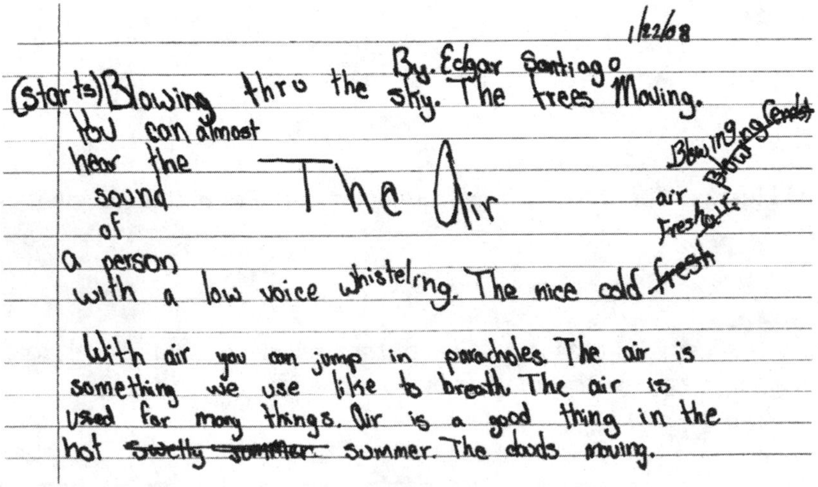
1/22/08
By. Edgar Santiago
(Starts) Blowing thro the sky. The trees Moving.
You can almost hear the sound of a person with a low voice whisteling. The nice cold fresh
The Air
air
Fresh air
With air you can jump in parachules. The air is something we use like to breath. The air is used for many things. Air is a good thing in the hot ~~sweetly summer~~ summer. The clouds moving.

Figure 10-7. "The Air" as Published

Blowing thru the sky. The trees moving.

You can   Relax

Almost   The Air   Blowing
Hear the   Air
Sound of   Fresh

A person with a low voice whistling. The nice cold

Jump in parachutes. Breathe. Air is a good thing. On
a hot sweaty summer day. The clouds. Moving

by Edgar S.

Through the publication circle, words and details are addcd, deleted, rearranged, and given a strong visual representation. Voice strengthens, genre is realized, and the visual presentation takes shape and contributes to meaning. At the conclusion of the publishing circle, every kid in the class has some writing to point to and be proud of. Every kid a published writer.

11

Smooth Operators:
Assessment, Evaluation,
and Management

The amount of writing students do should be far more than a teacher can evaluate.

—Tom Romano, *Clearing the Way*

How can we follow Romano's wise advice in our current United States of Assessment? Assessment can become the foe of learning when it takes on the dreaded connotations of the high-stakes test. But there are other ways to assess—measures that tell us, often in unobtrusive ways, how things are going for kids, their writing, and their writing circles.

Use kid-friendly assessment? Yes, we can.

Look at all the rich documentation of kids' thinking naturally provided by writing circles. Who needs a quiz? Every writing circle notebook holds an abundance of useful insight and information. There are the individual writing drafts, the regular think-back reflections, the list of new topics, the topics written about, the genres attempted, the peer responses, the publication role sheets, and the final revised and edited pieces. In addition, we have our own anecdotal records.

In assessing writing circles, it's useful to address the process as well as what kids learn. Involve kids by having them read through their writing circle notebook as a way of thinking about the writing circle process in general—what they liked as well as what things they want to improve. Discussion can then move from small groups (where kids share their observations) to the whole class, where you demonstrate how assessment is part of a process, not the final destination. You are looking for ways to make writing circles work better, be more successful, while also taking stock of and celebrating accomplishments.

Students have ranked writing circles at the top of the projects that we have worked on this year. It gave them the opportunity to grow as writers, work cooperatively (which is a developing concept for nine-year-olds), and collaboratively generate ideas for when they are writing independently during writers workshop.

—Jennifer McDonell

Self-Assessment Portfolios

Focus your assessment on demonstration rather than judgment, and shift responsibility for demonstration to kids. The goal is for kids to understand what they've learned and how they've learned it. As kids review their writing circle work, there are a number of artifacts they can draw on to demonstrate the extent and quality of their work. These artifacts include drafts, topic lists, think-backs, responsibilities assumed (timekeeper and first writer), evidence of different ways of responding, evidence of a variety of attempted genres and points of view, informal publication (such as golden sentences and gallery walks), and more formal publication (the publishing circle).

Have kids review their various artifacts and documentation and choose a manageable number to include in a portfolio. They can then share the contents of the portfolio with the teacher and classmates and talk about what they included and why. What do they notice about themselves as a writer? What would they point to as a good example of their "voice"? Can they point to a piece where they learned something about writing, where they grew as a writer? Based on what they have written in their writing circles, what new goals do they have for their writing? How many of their topics became writing circle topics? How many times did they share writing with the whole class? How many times were they the first writer? the timekeeper? *What did you learn about yourself as a writer?* There are so many fruitful questions—many of which kids can generate themselves.

Exit Slips

After kids have participated in a sufficient number of writing circle meetings to have informed opinions about the process, ask if they would recommend writing circles to other kids and why. Have them write their answer *anonymously* as an "exit slip"—usually an index card or a sticky note. Their exit comment can be as simple as yes or no, along with a brief rationale. Collect the exit slips at the end of class and read some back to kids the next day to frame a discussion. While effectiveness should not be determined by a vote, this raw example of democracy does provide a sense of how the writing circle experience is going for kids.

Comment Boards

Position three large sheets of poster paper in separate but convenient areas of the classroom. Label one sheet What I Like About Writing Circles, the second What I Dislike About Writing Circles, and the third What I Can Do to Make Writing Circles Work Even Better. Give each kid three post-it notes and ask them to write brief, anonymous comments related to each topic and then post them on the appropriate sheets. Color code the post-it notes for maximum efficiency and minimum confusion—say pink post-it notes for the "What I like about" comment board, blue for "What I dislike" and green for "What I can do." Kids, in groups, then move from sheet to sheet and take in the information. The ensuing reality-based discussion makes all the kids feel they own the problem-solving process. You can change the prompts to reflect specific situations. For example, if kids have chosen pieces to publish, headlines for the sheets might be I Chose This Piece to Publish Because, How I Feel About Spelling, and The Publication Role (Illustrator, Agent, Reader, Editor) I Liked Best.

Update Letters

This idea, suggested by Nancy Steineke, is similar to the exit slip but more broadly focused. Here is Nancy's invitation to her students:

> The goals of writing circles are to write frequently, provide an audience and positive feedback for all pieces, learn from your own writing, and listen to and discuss other kids' writing. Write me a letter updating me about how things are going. Tell me:
>
> *What you are learning about yourself as a writer:*
> How do you come up with a topic that everyone can write on?
> How do you go about your own writing?

Where do you get stuck?
What would you like to do better as a writer?

What's been interesting about hearing other people's writing:
What have you learned from listening to the other pieces?
How are your writing circle meetings going?
What's been working well?
What's something your circle could do to discuss one another's writing in more helpful ways?

Any important news in your life outside the writing circle you want to share?

The following are update letters written by the four students in Nancy Steineke's sophomore language arts class:

I'd like to say I know myself, but I don't. I'm beginning to get to know myself as a writer. I'm a selfish writer who likes to talk about me, myself, and I. To offer topics to everyone else, I think of topics that get everyone in, usually from previous discussions I've had. When it comes to my writing I often get stuck at the point of a fork in my brain; I can't decide which way to go from where I'm at. I'd like to choose the option that would interest, entertain, or inform the reader, but often end up just writing the one most interesting to me. Oh well, you can't please everyone I suppose.

What I like most about hearing other people's writing is that it's like a window into their mind. Everyone thinks in their own style, and you can see it by the way they write. I've learned things that I have in common with my classmates, and it makes talking to them much more comfortable. My circle's meetings are the bomb! It may seem exaggerated, but it's true. I like my group. We're all humorous people, so we work well together. I suppose if we had a serious member to keep us on track, we'd get more done. But you can't please everyone.
—Shannon C.

When I think of topics I try to relate to everyone in class. I think of the ideas in my head and figure out where they belong in the story. I get stuck usually around when I have to come up with my conclusion. I am learning that my stories sound a lot better in my head than on paper. I would like to be better at using more detail.

What's interesting is how you can relate with other students in your class. I have learned how to make my story come alive. Our writing circle meetings have been great and a lot of fun.

Some important news is that I have a dog.

—Tom G.

I've learned that as a writer I try to keep things light, and a bit funny. I've also learned a lot about my group through their stories, like that Jake is in a band and Shannon went to Catholic school. Something that hasn't been so easy is deciding on a topic. It usually takes us a while. I try to keep the option open so that one topic isn't makeup and another isn't skateboarding. It's been interesting to see the style my group members write in, which tells a lot about a person. Don't you think?

P.S. Can't wait for Homecoming!

—Stacey P.

I am learning about myself as a writer that I am better than I thought. I thought I was really bad at writing and that I would never be good. We come up with topics we can all write on by suggesting topics, then having everyone agree on one. When we pick one, I start writing by thinking of the topic and how it affects my life. Then I think it through and start writing. As a better writer, I would like to learn how to make my readers imagine that they are with me.

What's interesting about hearing other people's writing is that they are sometimes not as different from me as I think. Our writing circle meetings are going well, mainly because we are all communicating. Some things we can do to discuss our writing in more helpful ways is to get to know each other better. There is nothing new going on in my life.

—Jake A.

These update letters give Nancy a range of useful information about her students, their writing, and how writing circles are working for them. Nancy writes a brief affirmative response to each of the letters. Here's an example:

Shannon,

Good luck with merging your desires with pleasing your audience as well. Accomplishing that is a bit like walking a tightrope.

—S.

Self-Evaluations

Kids need to be able to take stock of their writing and their group work. Devising a simple form on which kids can jot down their thoughts helps guide that kind of response. See the example in Figure 11-1. The writing circle inventory (see Figure 11-2) takes a different focus while continuing to encourage kids to think about how they did as writers and group members.

Good-Faith Grades

Writing circles should definitely "count," because the process makes kids better writers. To have kids participate in a structure as substantial as writing circles and not have their work count toward a grade sends the message that writing circles aren't important. At the same time, attaching a grade to kids' work in writing circles risks turning them into the high-stakes, competitive-grading experience they are meant to counter.

One way to make writing circles count is to designate a percentage grade for what Tom Romano (1987) terms "good-faith participation": "We learn best, I think, through doing, through participating in good faith" (126). Participating in writing circles in good faith means being engaged in all aspects of the work—writing and sharing drafts, keeping good records, learning and practicing different responses, thinking of new topics, abetting the consensus process, helping the circle function by taking on responsibilities of first writer and timekeeper. It seems like a lot, but it is all interconnected and transparent. Through simple observation it's easy to see who's engaged and who is not. In classes too large for that kind of observation, the daily reflections provide additional accountability. *Good faith* means full credit or no credit. Either you're participating or you're not—and it's up to the individual kid to have enough work in their writing circle notebook to make the case for general participation.

HOW I DID

Your Name _____   Your Writing Circle _____

1. How did I help make my writing circle happen?

2. What kind of improvements have I noticed in my writing?

3. What did I do to help the other kids in my circle?

4. Did I learn anything from writing circles to use in the future?

WRITING CIRCLE INVENTORY

Your Name _____   Your Writing Circle _____

How many drafts did I write? _____

What are some favorite topics I wrote about?

What different kinds of writing did I try?

What was my biggest writing circle success?

   In my writing:

   In working with other kids in my circle:

What was the biggest writing circle problem?

   How did I try to solve it?

What have I learned about myself as a writer?

What have I learned about myself as a member of a group?

Is there anything else you want to say about being in writing circles?

Romano came up with a useful model for applying a grade to good-faith participation if you need to. Basically, "if a student completes the assignments they get a B, if they've done a good job they get an A, and if a participation has been something less than good faith, I lower the grade" (1987, 128).

When kids take one of their drafts through the publishing circle, there's the possibility of two grades—a good-faith grade (50%) and a grade for the published piece using the prevailing classroom writing rubric for finished pieces (50%).

Anecdotal Records

It is obvious every day during writing circles who's involved and who isn't. When you notice a kid isn't coming prepared with a draft and a new topic suggestion, isn't sharing, or simply isn't engaged in the process, all it usually takes is a brief conference to get the student back on track. As you move from one writing circle to the next, note something about each kid in that day's circle—something about their writing or topic choice, the way they responded or read aloud, whatever strikes you. By slightly adapting Daniels' literature circle observation record (2002, 190), you can capture a lot of information. See the example in Figure 11-3. (A blank version is provided in Figure 11-4.) Make anecdotal notes part of your own writing circle think-back reflection for the day rather than taking them during the writing circle meeting. During the writing circle meeting itself we concentrate on being good observers, and active listeners and responders.

WRITING CIRCLE OBSERVATIONS

Circle Name : *Nemo Crew*   Date: *11/05/0X*

NAME	PREPARED?	PARTICIPATED?	WRITING SKILL	SOCIAL SKILL
Edgar	+/−	+	+ Action verbs − No new topic	Asked to hear Shared last again
Elenzo	+	+	Repetition for effect	Encouraged Briana
Jermaine	−	+	− No draft	Took turns
Steve	+	−	Appeal to audience ("you")	No response First writer
Briana	+	+	Color detail ("emerald")	Good timekeeper

Possible minilessons:
    Edgar's verbs
    How to be a good timekeeper (Briana)

WRITING CIRCLE OBSERVATIONS

Circle Name: _____   Date: _____

NAME	PREPARED?	PARTICIPATED?	WRITING SKILL	SOCIAL SKILL

Possible minilessons:

Group Process Self-Evaluations

One of the benefits of writing circles is that kids learn to work together in small collaborative groups. It's useful for kids to describe their participation in this group process as part of their self-assessment. Provide opportunities for kids to reflect on and discuss how they worked together in their respective circles. What did they do to help their circle be successful? What could they have improved? What have they learned about working together in a group? Who in their circle would they point to as particularly important in achieving the consensus and collaboration that is at the heart of the writing circle process?

Reality Check

Another way to assess writing circles is to use the characteristics of writing circles as defined in Chapter 1 as the basis for a writing circle rubric (see Figure 11-5).

Every student a writer.

Reality Check Rubric

	YES	NO	UNSURE	EVIDENCE

In general, did writing circles:

Improve kids' attitudes toward writing?

Improve kids' ability to work together?

Make kids better writers?

Turn up the volume on kids' writing "voice?"

Teach kids different ways of responding
         to a topic?

         to one another's writing?

The Red Plastic Cup

> I gave each writing circle a red plastic cup with their writing circle name on it to place in the center of their table. When they are finished choosing someone in their group to share with the class, they turn their cup over—a simple (and very quiet) way to let me know they are ready to share. After the whole class has shared, the circles go back to work and choose a topic for the next day. When they are ready to share their topics for tomorrow, they again turn their cups over.
>
> —Jennifer McDonell

We all have a red plastic cup or its equivalent—our own ways of managing groups and group process. Management isn't about accountability, but accountability is often the key to smooth, efficient management. The red cups won't work if kids aren't accountable for using them. Accountability connects writing circle assessment and management. We want to know if kids are having difficulty of any kind, writing related or circle related.

Smooth management means circles happen the way they have been planned and there are ways to identify and solve problems. A key management structure in this regard is the writing circle notebook, with its daily think-back reflections. A look at the notebooks quickly tells us if kids are participating or if a specific writing circle is struggling.

The rotating roles of first writer and timekeeper help manage the writing circles day to day. The first writer gets the circle started by stepping up and reading their draft. Being the timekeeper doesn't sound all that important, yet the timekeeper's job is to get writing circle activities to happen on time, to make sure every kid has an opportunity to share a part or all of their writing, and that there's still time for response and choosing a new topic idea. One of the best things about the writing circle notebook and first writer and timekeeper roles is that they allow kids to share management responsibilities with you, giving them a sense of partnership and ownership in the process.

Writing Circle Variations

I love the way science writing circles are going—there has been diversity in responses to a topic, range of genre selection, and a lot of creativity.
—Melissa Schmidt

When you write about stuff in school it is always the traditional non-self-chosen topic writing. But with the writing circles you as a group discuss what scientific topics interest you most and then you could express your personal thoughts. It felt good to know that these are topics that I can relate to. It makes me feel like a teacher to that topic—sharing every detail that I know about fish or bacteria. And while sharing I can add more information from past experiences. And it also shows a creative side of you.
—A student

Content-Area Writing Circles

Writing circles provide a structure for students to explore content-area subject matter in their own way, to investigate, learn, and at the same time support one another as writers. The groups operate just as they do in language arts classrooms: kids name their writing circles, choose new topics through consensus, and write about the topic in whatever way they think will be effective. It's a way to get kids thinking and talking, using writing as learning—pure and simple and without penalty.

In Kennedy Middle School, the seventh-grade science writing circles were Oh Snap, Benchwarmers, Masterminds, Chick'n Nuggets, the ?'s, and Desperate House Guys. Their writing circle science topics included animal cruelty, cloning, holograms, diseases, evolution, and space.

The Benchwarmers decided to write about cloning and brought their drafts to their next circle meeting. One outlined the scientific steps of the cloning process. One described how to achieve 24/7 leisure by having a clone "do your homework and chores while you relax and have fun. Then the clone could go to school and you could chill on the couch all day." One student wrote a rant against cloning; another balanced the positive and negative aspects of cloning. The writing quality of these drafts was uneven, but there was much that was clear, forthright, and compelling. The ideas were there, ready to be sorted out and developed. The final Benchwarmer wrote the first part of a futuristic flashback (patterned after the lyrics of a country song by Brad Paisley):

Cloning

If I could write a letter to me, I'd send it back in time to myself at seven years. First I'd prove it's me by saying look under your bed, there's a jewelry box full of jewels you stole from Millie then.

I'd say these are the best times of your life. Your daddy's still cool, but over time from all that stress, he'll lose it just like that. Millie will still be givin' you love, hug her tight 'cause in seventeen months, she'll slip away so fast.

Go hug Aunt Jennie, every chance you can. Oh . . . you got so much going for you, going right, but I know at seven years it's hard to see past Friday night. You'll grow up and get a cute baby bro named Luke. Haley will move away. You'll get a boyfriend in sixth grade and take it slow. See you in the mirror, when you're a grown teen.

Meanwhile, the Masterminds were writing about holograms: "They will also be used as trademarks for Disney. Disney will then take over the media to control the brains of little children and bring them to their lair where they will sacrifice them to Mickey Mouse."

Through writing circles kids interact with content, learn from one another, and become stronger writers. The drafts the Chick'n Nuggets shared about their chosen topic, disease, showed the variety of genres writing circles encourage: a poem from a terminal patient's point of view; an exposé about the connection between disease, germs, and handling money; an extended definition of "zoonoses"; a lively description of the Black Plague; and a gruesome survey of the "Worst Diseases of All Time." In each draft the Chick'n Nuggets writing with the kind of confidence and authority mentioned by the student quoted at the start of this chapter, "like a teacher to that topic."

> In the math writing circles, kids solve multistep problems, write down their math reasoning, and then receive feedback about their communication of math reasoning from their writing circle peers.
>
> —Deborah Zaffiro

Whether in math, social studies, science, or some other content area, writing circles stand ready to help kids explore and connect learning through writing. In each circle, concepts are explored from as many points of view as there are kids. That the exploration happens through writing and is organized through kids' writing and response has significant social as well as academic payoffs, especially since kids need to write regularly in all content areas if they are to become stronger writers and thinkers.

Once writing circles are up and running and kids are comfortable with the process, they provide a way to jump-start other projects and investigations. Teachers frequently mention this type of *versatility* as one of the advantages of teaching and learning through writing circles.

> My kids are doing something slightly different right now. After reading and performing some plays and two-part poetry, they wanted to write their own play. We brainstormed several topics, and they selected (as a class) the one they liked best. We then discussed the plot of the play, what they would like the major action to be, and who the characters should be and assigned parts. Next, we summarized each scene and identified which characters carried the action. Since there were four scenes, I divided the class into four writing circles and they are writing the play. As I have joined the groups randomly, the conversation, arguments, and agreements have been really delightful.
>
> —Joan LoPresti

Teacher Writing Circles

As a means of professional development, writing circles offer educators a way to build community, learn how to collaborate, and come to a larger understanding of writing and how to help kids become stronger writers.

Forming their own writing circles gives teachers a good demonstration of how they work and how the circles can benefit their students.

Teacher writing circles take a variety of formats: online, in a school, throughout a district, teachers from different schools, teachers from the same school, teachers at the same grade level, preservice teachers, teachers in summer institutes. Three teacher writing groups sponsored by the National Writing Project met for years with the goal of "using writing and related collaborative learning processes to better understand classroom practice" (Robbins, Seaman, Yancey, and Yow 2006).

Just as many teachers form their own literature circles before introducing them to students, a writing circle of teachers can meet before and/or concurrently with those in the classroom. Teachers who participate in teacher writing circles are much more comfortable sharing their writing and modeling the process for kids. Teacher writing circles are a place for teachers to understand through doing and reflecting on that doing—a place for teachers to see themselves as writers.

If you are in a teacher writing circle, present a fishbowl demonstration of one of your sessions for other teachers and school administrators. Looking into the fishbowl will give your colleagues a clearer sense of what writing circles are as well as inviting them to become more involved.

Teachers name their circles and follow the basic writing circle rhythm of writing, sharing, responding, and reflecting. In their circles, teachers practice different response minilessons, choose new writing ideas through consensus, and think back on the implications of their own writing and how they teach writing. Teachers' writing topics occasionally focus on curriculum, educational issues, and inclusive classrooms, but more often they are similar to the kind of open-ended topics kids choose: childhood memories, drinking coffee, crying, favorite movies, favorite foods, embarrassing moments, and physical ailments. And the writing that teachers share demonstrates the range of approaches and points of view writing circles encourage—for kids *and* teachers.

> Our learning team wrote about crying. The results included a poem about different experiences that caused a person to cry, a scientific examination of what the eyes do when one cries, a mother's memory of a blood-curdling scream of a child, and a narrative reflection about crying while teaching a class.
> —Deborah Zaffiro

Teacher writing circles change many teachers' view of themselves as writers and as teachers of writing. Being in a writing circle (re)establishes the importance of sharing writing, reignites the joy of writing, and helps teachers reflect on their teaching through the lens of the circle experience.

A teacher writing circle, the *Explorers,* continue their written adventure.

Epilogue   The End Is Also the Beginning

We've named our writing circles. We are the:

Peanut Butter Jellies
Ghost Writers
Cupid Shuffle
Salad
D4L (Down for Life)
Purple Hoopdiddy Loopders

I'm looking forward to building on what I learned from writing circles last year. Guess that's one of the things about circles—the end is also the beginning.

Thumbs up for writing circles!

Book Study Suggestions

Writing Circles: Kids Revolutionize Workshop
Jim Vopat

A *Writing Circles* study group offers opportunities to:

- Read, question, discuss, adapt, apply, and reflect on the ideas from *Writing Circles*.
- Participate in a writing circle and experience the approach.
- Plan and problem-solve with colleagues who have started or want to start writing circles with their students.

There are as many ways to structure a study group as there are site specific variables, like amount of meeting time available and frequency of meetings. Regardless of these variations, key to success is a welcoming climate in which you feel free and safe to participate in the ongoing conversation and exchange of ideas—not to mention writing. This is the same kind of learning community we strive for in writing circles with kids.

Two principles of the National Writing Project inform the *Writing Circle* study groups we've been part of. The first is that teachers are the best teachers of teachers. The second is that we truly learn by doing. "Teachers teaching teachers" honors the professionalism, judgment, and good will of teachers. Regardless of grade level or content area, all teachers are united in the same goal as writing circles: improved student writing. We trust teachers to take away from the group session what they see as useful and valuable and adapt and evaluate strategies from their unique perspectives. This means that we don't just want to talk about ideas, we want to try them out ourselves, both in the study group and in our own classrooms. This kind of first-hand knowledge allows for deeper understanding and conversation as we talk about how to implement writing circles with students of any age.

As you plan your book study, here are a few other things that can help make the experience more engaging and meaningful.

Form a Diverse Group: Circumstances permitting, encourage teachers from different grade levels and content specialties to participate. Such diversity deepens conversation, increases understanding, and creates a common language across grades, buildings, and even districts.

Watch Group Size: A good number for individual writing circles is 4–6 participants, and that's also a good size for lively democratic discussions. If you have a larger base group, split the time between smaller writing circle groups and larger whole group discussion and decision-making.

Design a Recurrent Format: One way to organize recurrent book study meetings would be to design a format to reflect the principles and approaches described in the book:

- An opening Building Community activity.
- Conversation about the book based on reading and chapter questions/suggestions.
- Conversation about classroom writing instruction as seen through the chapters of the book—including time for teachers who have started writing circles in their classrooms to share their observations about the process.
- Form writing circles. Writing circles meet for the first time as part of the discussion of Chapter 3, and then continue to meet for at least 20 minutes as part of each subsequent book study session.
- Closure. End each book study on time, but not before plans and expectations for the next meeting are clear—including schedule, reading, writing circle drafts, and classroom applications.

Study Questions/Suggestions: Are simply that—not a curriculum. The best study questions are yours. Questions/suggestions are meant to trigger additional questions/suggestions and launch conversation. Here are some ways of using the questions:

- Place 3 or 4 of the suggested questions in an envelope and randomly pull them out for discussion.
- Jot down one "burning question" (Chapter 7, p. 95) based on your reading and bring it to the book study meeting. Collect these "burning questions" and make the envelope-draw from them.

- Start with one big question that comes from the Agenda Building (see next idea).

Create an Agenda: Prior or during the first book study meeting, list what you hope to gain from being in *this* study group. Combine agenda items and prioritize. Eliciting an agenda obligates the group to follow up on it. Take one agenda item at a time, and let it frame the conversation.

Encourage Text Annotation and Use of a Writing Circle Notebook: Annotate sections of the book you want to talk about. You can do this by underlining, highlighting, making marginal comments—as long as you own your book. If you're using a borrowed copy, model what it might be like to read books from the classroom library by using sticky-notes for the same purpose. Kids in writing circles document their participation and process by keeping a writing circle notebook, and it makes sense for you to keep such a notebook as well (see Chapter 6, p. 85). The writing circle notebook can contain your reading notes, observations, writing topic lists, and, once writing circles are established, drafts, and regular think-back reflections (Figures 2-1 and 3-2).

Include Opportunities for Reflection: Leave some time at the end of study sessions to write about what you have observed and how this experience might influence the way you teach writing. A simple format might be:

What I've observed:

How this observation might influence my teaching:

How I can follow up on this observation:

In addition, as noted above, once writing circles are formed, you can also complete regular think-back reflections as part of your writing circle meetings.

Democracy Now: Share leadership of the book study sessions. In a leaderless group, every member is equally responsible for the group's success. If you decide to have weekly leaders, find an easy process for rotating responsibilities. Responsibilities could include Book Study Facilitator, Question Master, and Writing Circle Facilitator.

Honor Group Dynamics: Periodically reflect on the group dynamics and what can be done to welcome everyone to the conversation. As in any conversation, be realistic as to how they often diverge only to come back to the point.

Form Writing Circles and "try out" the writing, community building, and minilesson activities: Participating in ongoing writing circles allows you to view classroom practice through authentic experience. Katie Wood Ray has shown us how important the connection is between our own writing experiences and classroom practice, how our own experiences with writing inform the way we teach writing (*What You Know by Heart,* Heinemann, 2002). Taking part in a writing circle while preparing to or inaugurating them in the classroom provides a very serendipitous opportunity to unite and live theory and practice. Writing circles can form as part of the discussion of Chapter 3, Getting Started. Writing circles then continue to meet as a regular part of subsequent study group sessions—becoming publishing circles in conjunction with reading Chapters 10, 11, and 12.

Starting with the initial study group meeting, we want to diffuse your anxiety about writing and sharing your writing. Writing circles exist to alleviate such anxiety and rehabilitate the writing wounded. *Writing Circles* is definitely a "how-to book," and you are encouraged to demonstrate and experience the community building, writing, and minilesson activities during sessions.

Get Off to a Good Start: Some snacks, an agenda, and an opening community building activity from Chapter 4. A comfortable place to have conversation and write—preferably chairs around circular tables. Writing circle notebooks and a copy of the book.

Celebrate: Take time to enjoy each other's participation, writing, and points of view.

What Would Make You Return: Think about the book study in terms of what would make you want to return. The treats, the space, the camaraderie, the community building, the sharing of writing, the conversation, the ideas, the dreams, the questionings, and the spirit of everyone working together to make writing better.

NOTE: Being comfortable writing quick sustained drafts and feeling at ease with each other are important to the success of writing circles. Being at ease with writing and each other doesn't happen immediately—whether we are talking about kids or adults. So even though the Building Community and Writeable Moments are later in the book (Chapters 4 and 5), it's a good idea to incorporate community building and brief informal writing in the initial meetings of the study group, so that when writing circles start—concurrent with the discussion of Chapter 3—participants will look forward to writing and sharing their writing.

In other words, everyone is encouraged to read ahead, and then revisit the specific reading when it is scheduled for discussion. Please enjoy *Writing Circles*, the book and the experience.

Chapter 1
The Tao of Writing Circles

One of the goals of this chapter is to provide the context and make the argument for writing circles. As part of the discussion, try one of the Building Community activities from Chapter 4 and some brief non-stressful writing—like freewriting (Chapter 5, p. 69). Use your writing circle notebook for the writing.

1. Tao cannot be expressed but it can be known. The title of the chapter provides an opportunity to talk about the connection between "doing" and "learning," "experience" and "understanding."
2. What about the "writing wounded?" When you think about your classroom, how does the term "writing wounded" apply? What about you? Do you belong to the "writing wounded" as well? As a member of the study group, how do you feel when told there will be opportunities to write and share your writing?
3. Basically, writing circles depend on a positive group dynamic. How prepared are your students for productive collaborative group work? Talk about it.

4. "Writing response groups are largely under-utilized in classrooms." When you think about writing in your classroom, how do writing response groups fit in?
5. "Increasingly we lead collaborative lives—and that includes our writing." What kind of collaborative writing experiences are available for kids in your classroom?
6. Have you been in an adult writing group? If so, how does that experience inform what you expect will happen in writing circles?
7. How important is student choice and small group collaboration to learning?
8. How would you rate the "writing confidence" of students you teach? How do you know?

Chapter 2

The Basics

1. Continue to incorporate at least one building community and one writeable moment activity into the study group meeting.
2. Which of writing circles' 13 basic steps do you feel will pose challenges for your students? Which parts of the process do you feel students will readily embrace?
3. In writing circles kids write numerous uncorrected drafts. How do you think kids will respond to this aspect of writing circles? What about parents? School administrators? You?
4. How do you feel about "good faith effort" as a basis for assessment and grades?
5. "We need to teach kids positive ways to talk to one another about their writing." Do students you teach have "positive ways" for discussing one another's writing? How did they learn them?
6. When kids share their writing in small groups in class, do they know how to ask for the kind of information they need to make their writing better?
7. Ongoing reflection is one of writing circles' recurrent structures. What opportunities for students to "reflect" on their learning already occur in your teaching? How important is reflection to learning?

8. The chapter concludes with a series of Frequently Asked Questions. What would be your FAQ? Write your FAQ on an index card. Bring this FAQ to the book study and exchange cards so that everyone has someone else's FAQ. Read the FAQ, write an answer on the reverse side of the index card, and return to sender. Circulate the cards and read. This leads to a wide ranging discussion. The FAQ's themselves can serve as an agenda for future meetings and reading.

Chapter 3

Getting Started

Chapter 3 describes how to introduce writing circles to students (Day One). It's the assumption of this study guide that participants will form writing circles as part of the discussion of Chapter 3, and that writing circle meetings will continue as part of the ongoing study group. If anyone has started writing circles in their classrooms, give them regular opportunities to share their observations about how the writing circle process is going for their students.

1. Consistent with the process described in Chapter 3, come prepared with three writing ideas written on index cards. After the writing circles are formed (strategies on pp. 36–37) each circle chooses a writing topic (using the stack the deck strategy variation (p. 38), names their writing circle, and identifies the next circle meeting's first writer and timekeeper. If there is more than one writing circle, then they need to share their names and writing topic with the base group. If there's time, write briefly about your topic, and complete the abbreviated think-back reflection (p. 41).

2. There is a lot to talk about after experiencing the first writing circle, so leave time and provide a structure for everyone to share observations. How is this going to work for students?

Chapter 3 also describes the second writing circle meeting in which "the recurrent writing circle structure becomes fully operational" (p. 42). Schedule this second writing circle for the next study group meeting. At that time you will have written a draft in your writing circle notebook; also jot down a new topic suggestion. Either the facilitator or a volunteer can model the "one thing I like about your writing" response minilesson (p. 42) before writing circles reform. Timekeepers and first writers have been identified from the previous writing circle meeting. Once the writing circles have formed and the timekeepers have figured how much time everyone has to share, the first writer begins by reading their writing aloud to the circle. After sharing and response, come to a consensus about the next writing circle topic, and identify the next circle meeting's timekeeper and first writer. If there is more than one writing circle, each circle then re-states their name and their new topic to the entire book study group. This second writing circle meeting concludes by completing the Think-Back form (Figure 2-1). One way to expedite discussion is to pass these completed think-backs around and read what individuals have written, and then talk about what you observe. What are the implications for students?

Chapter 4
Building Community

1. It seems appropriate to try at least one new building community experience from this chapter with students. How did this go? If possible bring some student samples to share with colleagues.
2. It seems equally appropriate to have someone demonstrate one of the building community activities for the study group. How did this go? Implications for your classroom?
3. How can you tell if the climate in your classroom is "too hot," "too cold," or "just right" for writing circles?
4. What differences might you expect to notice between a classroom in which community has been nourished, and one where it has not?
5. Do you agree with Peter Johnson that "in productive classrooms, teachers don't just teach children skills; they build emotionally and relationally healthy learning communities?" What makes a learning community "healthy?"
6. What connections do you see between the building community strategies in this chapter and writing circle success?
7. Writing circles continue to meet.
8. If you have started writing circles in your classrooms, continue to share observations about how it's going.

Chapter 5

Writeable Moments

1. As a way of focusing discussion, try out one of the chapter's "writeable moments"—like personal metaphor—to experience and share in the study group.
2. Do you agree that taking the "pressure" off writing can lead to better writing?
3. How do you respond to Peter Elbow's statement that "freewriting" is the best all around practice in writing I know" (p. 69).
4. What kind of opportunities do kids have to write "back and forth about compelling issues" in your classroom?
5. Try some new low-risk writing activities from this chapter with students. Bring some sample student responses to the study group and talk about the relative merits of this kind of writing. One way to spread the word is to go around the whole group quickly—with each participant stating a writeable moment they used in class and how it worked.
6. Writing circles continue to meet.
7. If you've started writing circles in your classrooms, continue to share observations about how it's going.

Chapter 6

The Writing Circle Notebook

1. Hopefully, you have your own writing circle notebook and experience to bring to the conversation. If your students are also engaged in writing circles, bring some student notebooks to serve as a real-time lens through which to view the writing circle notebook process.
2. "The writing circle notebook is also a resource kids use to understand themselves better as writers" (p. 87). Reviewing some of the sample notebooks (of teachers and students), how useful do you feel the notebook can be to helping students understand themselves as writers?
3. How well does the think-back process work for you and for students?

4. What modifications of the think-back template would you make for your students?

5. Writing circles continue to meet.

6. If you have started writing circles in your classroom, continue to share observations about how it's going.

Chapter 7

Writing Circle Minilessons

1. Which writing circle minilessons come to mind when you read Lucy Calkins' statement, "What is the one thing I can suggest or demonstrate that might help the most?" For you? For your students?

2. Is it true that some kids edit their "voice" from their writing? If so, what factors are at play?

3. As teachers, how do we decide which writing circle minilessons will be productive and when to introduce them?

4. Demonstrate one of the writing circle minilessons for the rest of the participants in the study group.

5. In your writing circle listen for instances of strong voice in the writing you hear and share your observations for the response part of the writing circle meeting.

6. If there is more than one writing circle, each circle shares some of their writing with the larger base group. After each circle has shared, try some different ways of celebrating (p. 112). If the base group is the same as the writing circle, practice a different celebration response after each draft is read aloud. How do you keep these mini-celebrations from taking over the writing and diffusing meaningful response?

7. Fishbowl conferences are versatile, engaging, and fun to do and watch. When your writing circle meets, be on the lookout for a good writing circle minilesson to fishbowl. Choose one and fishbowl it.

8. Continue to provide time to share observations as to how writing circles are working for students.

Chapter 8

Positive Response

1. Think about how students in general respond to each other's writing. What do they say to each other? How did they learn these responses?
2. How did you learn different ways of responding to writing? What are they?
3. Re-read the Responder Roles from the South Coast Writing Project (Figure 8-1, p. 119). How do you feel these guidelines will work with students? What adaptations would you make for kids you teach?
4. What's your take on the paradox stated by Peter Elbow and Pat Belanoff that when sharing writing "the reader is always right; yet the writer is always right" (121)?
5. The chapter describes ten low-risk ways for kids to respond to each other's writing. One way to understand the differences between responses is to view a single student draft through all ten responses—such as the responses to the "Darkness" student draft on pp. 127–28. Choose a common student draft (from the book or from a student with permission) and assign different ways to respond to members of the study group. Try to make sure that all ten response strategies are represented. Name the response you are using and write it down on a card or sticky note. Then read through the student draft and write (or draw for "Sketch It") the response on the card or note. Pass the responses around and see the variety of positive possibilities.
6. Demonstrate a "response" minilesson to set up the day's writing circle. Choose a response strategy that can then be used during the writing circle meeting.
7. Writing circles meet.
8. Make time to share observations about how writing circles are working with students.

Chapter 9
Enjoyable Ways Kids Can Share Writing with the Whole Class

1. This chapter focuses on the transition from the individual circles to the whole class sharing of new topics and some writing from the circles with the whole group.
   - Why is it important for this kind of "reporting out" to take place?
   - What benefits are there to restating the writing circle name and new topic for the entire group or class?
   - What are the benefits to sharing some writing from each circle whole group or class?
   - Is it realistic to have a brief class-wide celebration after each writing circle shares? What are the possible benefits? What could go wrong?

2. What style and craft minilesson would you base on the golden sentences from the Femme Lattes (p. 135)?

3. For today's writing circle meeting, have the writer choose the type of response they want from the group before they read their draft aloud. How important is it for the writer to choose the response they need from their writing circle?

4. It's not necessary to choose a new writing topic for the next meeting. Instead, you will be searching through all your drafts looking for possible writing "kernels" to grow through the publication circle.

5. Try out one of the whole class sharing strategies: Let Your Light Shine, I Hear a Symphony, Post It, Open Mike, Gallery Walk, Golden Sentence, Read-Around, Found Poem, First Impression/ Final Impression. Be sensitive to the reality that some of the sharing strategies take more time than others. Use the results of this sharing to focus conversation on the whole class sharing aspect of the writing circle dynamic.

6. Continue to share observation about how writing circles are working in the classrooms.

Chapter 10
Publishing Circles

1. The chapter describes the transition from writing circles to publishing circles. The best basis for a study of the chapter is for you to engage in the same process. That means scheduling time to review all your drafts and choose the "writing kernel" you want to explore more fully. Share the kernel with your circle and discuss the next steps for developing and revising it. The process of choosing the writing kernel provides an opportunity to reflect on and discuss the benefits and challenges of moving a draft forward to a finished piece.

2. After you've had time to revise the writing kernel (either within the actual study group meeting time or on your own), work with the agent, illustrator, reviewer, editor, and author role sheets on pp. 143–150. If time is limited, the role sheets can be divided so that each role sheet is completed at least once by someone in the circle. This leads to a more informed discussion of the value of the distinctly different conferences described in the chapter. For example, whoever completes the Agent conference and role sheet can talk about that role and the value of the resulting information elicited through the Agent conference—and similarly for the other conferences and roles. The point is to have sufficient first-hand experience with the four conferences and five role sheets to have an informed and reality-based conversation about the whole process. This is the time to bring classroom experiences using the roles to the conversation.

3. "The problem with 'role sheets' in general is their tendency to become mechanical" (p. 138). Given your (and your students') experience with the publication circle role sheets, do you feel they successfully resist this "tendency?"

4. Do you feel the publication circle roles—agent, illustrator, reviewer, editor, and author—provide sufficient range of perspectives and information to make the process meaningful and productive?

5. "Adapt these roles to reflect the realities of writing in your classroom" (p.142). In what ways would you revise the roles and/or role sheets in your classroom?

6. The scheduling realities of your study group may make it difficult to fully complete the publication circle, especially fully conferencing, and then revising and editing the writing into final form. Make adjustments, but don't skip opportunities to experience and share observations about the publication circle roles and conference process.

7. How important is it for students to publish some of their writing? Are there situations in which publication becomes a negative? Explain the negative dynamic.

8. How well do students make the transition from writing circles to publishing circles? What are some observations from classrooms?

Chapter 11
Smooth Operators: Assessment, Evaluation, and Management

1. How do you feel about Tom Romano's statement that "the amount of writing students do should be far more than a teacher can evaluate?" What are the implications of this statement for how you teach writing?

2. Choose a couple of the assessment strategies described in the chapter to complete, share, and discuss.

3. Which of the assessment strategies do you feel would work best with your students? What adaptations for your students would you make?

4. Do you feel the described assessment strategies are sufficient measurements for the writing circle/publication circle process?

5. How comfortable are you now with the concept of "good-faith grades" (p. 158)? Have your opinions changed from when you first read about this good faith approach? How are students responding to the "good faith grade" concept? Colleagues? Administrators? Parents?

6. "We all have a red plastic cup or its equivalent—our own ways of managing groups and group process" (p. 166). Share your favorite "red cup" strategy.

7. Publication circles continue to meet to experience the conferencing roles and strategies described in Chapter 10.

8. Continue to share student writing and publishing circle observations from classrooms.

Chapter 12
Writing Circle Variations

1. What advantages do you see to implementing writing circles in the content areas?
2. Do you feel that writing circles in the content areas will increase student learning and improve writing skills? What is your reasoning?
3. How can administrators and colleagues gain writing circle "buy in" from content area teachers?
4. Now that you are near the conclusion of the book study group, if there's interest, discuss how it would be possible to establish an ongoing teacher/administrator writing circle. What's necessary to make it happen?
5. Author and educational keynote speaker Doug Reeves has said that if teachers and administrators return to the classroom or school office from a professional development experience and nothing happens, then the "adult learning experience was nothing more than an illusion, a mirage of improved practice in the middle of a desert of indifference." What needs to happen to make sure that the meaning and experience of this writing circle study group will prove to be more than a "mirage?"
6. When you think about writing circles, what do you envision for you, your students, and your school?
7. How will teachers who plan to implement writing circles (or are already doing so) going to stay connected for support and dissemination of information?
8. If this is the final book study group meeting, celebrate some writing from everyone using one of the whole-class sharing strategies from Chapter 9 (such as displaying a golden sentence from everyone or a section of each person's writing as a gallery walk).
9. As you take leave of each other, remember, to quote *Writing Circle's* epilogue, that "the end is also the beginning."

Thanks and Works Cited

To teachers who believe every student is a writer and all the students who prove them right. To everyone at Heinemann for their commitment and support—especially Patty Adams' fine art of production. To Harvey "Smokey" Daniels for writing *Literature Circles*, my mentor text. To Joan LoPresti, Jane Borden, Matt Stark, Abby Plummer, and Deb Zaffiro for inviting me into their classrooms.   To Elise Riepenhoff for her friendship and leadership. To Nancy Steineke, mentor teacher, for her irrepressible spirit, vision, and just-in-time advice. To Elaine Daniels for reading early and staying late. To Peter Elbow, Mary Rose O'Reilley, Stephanie Harvey, and Nancie Atwell for pointing the way.   To Bob Miller for everything.

Chapter 1

6 + 1 Trait writing at www.nwrel.org/assessment/department.

Bandura, Albert. 1982. "Self-Efficacy Mechanism and Human Agency." *American Psychologist* 84: 191–215.

Calkins, Lucy. 1994. *The Art of Teaching Writing*. Portsmouth, NH: Heinemann.

Daniels, Harvey. 2002. *Literature Circles*. Portland, ME: Stenhouse.

Elbow, Peter. 1997. "High Stakes and Low Stakes in Assigning and Responding to Writing." In *New Directions for Teaching and Learning,* ed. Peter Elbow and Deane Sorcinelli 69. San Francisco: Jossey-Bass.

Fountas, Irene, and Gay Su Pinnell. 2000. *Guiding Readers and Writers (Grades 3–6): Teaching Comprehension, Genre, and Content Literacy.* Portsmouth, NH: Heinemann.

Gere, Anne Ruggles. 1987. *Writing Groups: History, Theory, and Implications.* Carbondale, IL: Southern Illinois University Press.

Knudsen, R. 1995. "Writing Experiences, Attitudes, and Achievement of First to Sixth Graders." *Journal of Educational Research* 89(2): 90–97.

Routman, Regie. 1991. *Invitations*. Portsmouth, NH: Heinemann.

Zaffiro, Deborah. 2006. "Writing Groups as a Tool for Improving Student Writing." (unpublished report). Milwaukee Public Schools.

Thanks to . . .

Both Lucy Calkins and Ralph Fletcher employ the "seed bed" metaphor to describe writing growth.

Chapter 2

Graves, Donald H. 1985. "All Children Can Write." Reprinted on LD OnLine. www.ldonline.org/article/6204.

Zemelman, Steve, Harvey Daniels, and Arthur Hyde. 1999. *Best Practice: New Standards for Teaching and Learning in America's Schools.* Portsmouth, NH: Heinemann.

Chapter 3

Brompton, S. 2008. "Daily Horoscope." *New York Post*, April 4: 58, www.nypost.com.

Steineke, Nancy. 2002. *Reading and Writing Together: Collaborative Literacy in Action*. Portsmouth, NH: Heinemann.

Chapter 4

Cisneros, Sandra. 1984. *The House on Mango Street*. New York: Random House.

Johnston, Peter H. 2004. *Choice Words*. York, ME: Stenhouse.

Proust's answers to the two questionnaires he took can be found at http://pagesperso-orange.fr/chabrieres/marcelproustquestionnaire.html.

Smith Magazine, ed. 2008. *Not Quite What I Was Planning: Six-Word Memoirs by Writers Famous and Obscure*. New York: HarperCollins.

Van Allsburg, Chris. 1984. *The Mysteries of Harrison Burdick*. Boston: Houghton Mifflin.

Thanks to . . .

Diversity Circle adapted from Lucy Ware and the Western Pennsylvania Writing Project, University of Pittsburgh.

Magee, Bronagh and the ESL Blogcast for Chain Stories for classroom pointers.

Headline News adapted from Peterson, Art, ed. 2003. 30 *Ideas for Teaching Writing*. Berkeley, CA: National Writing Project.

Six word memoir writing extension activities inspired by Rochelle Melander.

Chapter 5

Atwell, Nancie. 1998. *In the Middle*. Portsmouth, NH: Heinemann.

Barrett, Grant. 2007. *Buzzwords* 2007: All We Are Saying. *New York Times*, December 23.

Calkins, Lucy. 1994. *The Art of Teaching Writing*. Portsmouth, NH: Heinemann.

Elbow, Peter. 1981. *Writing with Power*. New York: Oxford University Press.

Fletcher, Ralph. 1996. *Breathing In, Breathing Out: Keeping a Writer's Notebook*. Portsmouth, NH: Heinemann.

Graves, Donald. 1983. *WRITING: Teachers and Children at Work*. Portsmouth, NH: Heinemann.

Lansky, Bruce. www.gigglepoetry.com. Accessed April, 15, 2008.

Routman, Regie. 1991. *Invitations*. Portsmouth, NH: Heinemann.

Thanks to . . .

Personal Metaphor adapted from a handout from South Coast Writing Project, University of California Santa Barbara.

"I Am From . . . " adapted from the poet George Ella Lyon, http://georgeellalyon.com. Further refined for the classroom by contributing teacher, Joan LoPresti.

Chapter 7

6 + 1 Trait writing, www.nwrel.org/assessment/department www.nwrel.org/assessment/scoringpractice.php

Atwell, Nancie. 2002. *Lessons That Change Writers*. Portsmouth, NH: Heinemann.

Calkins, Lucy. 1994. *The Art of Teaching Writing*. Portsmouth, NH: Heinemann.

Daniels, Harvey, and Nancy Steineke. 2004. *Mini-Lessons for Literature Circles*. Portsmouth, NH: Heinemann.

Fletcher, A. 2002. Fist to Five Consensus-Building Strategy. In *FireStarter Youth Empowerment Curriculum: Participant Guidebook*. Olympia, WA: Common Action.

Harvey, Stephanie. 1998. *Nonfiction Matters: Reading, Writing, and Research in Grades 3–8*. York, ME: Stenhouse.

Hoyt, Linda. 2000. *Snapshots: Literacy Minilessons Up Close*. Portsmouth, NH: Heinemann.

Ray, Katie Wood, with Lisa Cleveland. 2004. *About the Authors*. Portsmouth, NH: Heinemann.

Rief, Linda. 1992. *Seeking Diversity*. Portsmouth, NH: Heinemann.

Steineke, Nancy. 2002. *Reading and Writing Together: Collaborative Literacy in Action*. Portsmouth, NH: Heinemann.

Thanks to . . .

Ways to celebrate writing as a class inspired by contributing teacher, Jody Henderson-Sykes.

Annotated Neighborhood Map activity from the South Coast Writing Project, University of California, Santa Barbara.

Chapter 8

Edwards, L.H. 2005. "Law School Writing Without Teachers: Participating in an Advanced WritingGroup." www.law.mercer.edu/academics/legal_writing/certificate/advanced writinggroup.pdf

Elbow, Peter, and P. Belanoff. 2000 (3rd edition). *Sharing and Reponding*. Boston: McGraw Hill.

Elrod, Anne. "Reflections on an Online Teachers Writing Group." *The Quarterly*, 24(1).

Strategies for low-stakes response:

Elbow, Peter. 1997. Specific Uses and Benefits of Low Stakes Writing. In *Assigning and Responding to Writing in the Disciplines,* ed. M.D. Sorcinelli and P. Elbow. San Francisco: Jossey-Bass.

Thanks to . . .

Peter Elbow and Pat Belanoff devised the terminology and concept of "pointing" and "sayback."

Sketch It was inspired by Jerome Harste's "sketch to stretch" reading strategy.

Joan Cotich, Cheryl Armstrong, and The Santa Barbara Writing Group of the South Coast Writing Project for their excellent handouts on the work of Peter Elbow, writing groups, and response.

Chapter 9

Thanks to . . .

I first learned about "Gallery Walk" from Nancy Doda at the Walloon Institute.

Chapter 10

Haddon, Mark. 2005. *The Curious Incident of the Dog in the Night-Time*. New York: Random House.
Maimon, Elaine. 1985. Assignment. In *What Makes Writing Good*, edited by W. Coles and J. Vopat. Lexington, MA: D.C. Heath and Co.

Chapter 11

Daniels, Harvey. 2002. *Literature Circles*. Portland, ME: Stenhouse.
Romano, Tom. 1987. *Clearing the Way: Working with Teenage Writers*. Portsmouth, NH: Heinemann.

Thanks to . . .

Post It strategy inspired by contributing teacher, Elise Riepenhoff, director of the Milwaukee Writing Project, Carroll University, Waukesha, Wisconsin.
Nancy Steineke created the Update Letter and protocol. Nancy's students were willing to share their response.

Chapter 12

Robbins, Sara, G. Seaman, Kathleen B. Yancey, and Dede Yow. 2006. *Teachers' Writing Groups*. Kennesaw, GA: Kennesaw State University Press.

Index